Knits
&
Pieces

A KNITTING MISCELLANY

Knits & Pieces

DANIELLE HOLKE

UNICORN

First published by Unicorn
an imprint of the Unicorn Publishing Group LLP, 2017
101 Wardour Street
London W1F 0UG

www.unicornpublishing.org

10 9 8 7 6 5 4 3 2 1

ISBN 978-1-910787-63-2

Cover design Unicorn Publishing Group
Typeset by Vivian@Bookscribe
Illustrations by Collin Douma

Printed and bound in Slovenia

Contents

1. The History of Knitting

"I turn strings into things, what's your superpower?"

What is Knitting?

Simply put, knitting is the process by which one uses two or more needles to manipulate yarn into a series of interconnected loops to create a stretchy fabric. A fairly modern invention, the term "to knit" was not added to the English language until the 1400s. The word "knit" itself is thought to be derived from the word knot, a word that likely originates from the Dutch verb *knutten*, which is close to the Old English *cnyttan*, which means to knot. Got that?

Knitting is thought to have its nascent roots in the ancient method of knotting fishing nets. It's believed that around 200 CE, Arabian fishermen knotted nets to be able to catch and carry more fish. Eventually this practice led to knitting as we know it today.

Other ancient techniques for producing fabrics from thread include weaving, crochet and nalbinding (also known as naalbinding, nalebinding) … more on that last one later.

Knitting differentiates itself from other fabric-producing techniques in several ways:

☆ Knitted fabric is produced from one continuous string as opposed to weaving which uses two sets of threads.

☆ To produce knitted fabric, one uses two needles, as opposed to nalbinding or crochet, both of which use only one instrument.

☆ Knitted fabric is created from interconnected loops, the full length of the working thread is not worked through the loop as it is in nalbinding.

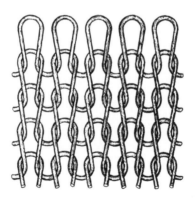

A diagram showing the interconnected loops

What's the difference between knitting, crochet, weaving and nalbinding? (See chart on page 10.)

KNITTING	CROCHET	WEAVING	NALBINDING
Uses two needles to produce a set of interconnected loops from one continuous string.	One hook is used to create work formed only of loops, never involving the free end of the thread.	Woven fabric is produced by interlacing two separate sets of threads.	Uses one needle and involves passing the full length of the working thread through each loop.

FUN FACT: Although no one knows for certain, it's generally accepted that the technique of knitting is younger than weaving and nalbinding, but older than crochet.

The History of Knitting

*"To knit or not to knit.
Now that's a silly question."*

Where Did It Originate?

No one knows! Well, no one knows for certain, that is. Up until recently, it was believed that a textile fragment discovered in the 1930s by a French-American team of archaeologists at the ancient Syrian city of Dura Europos was knitted. Thought to have been produced in approximately 256 CE, the fragment, which is currently housed at Yale University, was later proven to have been made using the nalbinding technique.

The "Dura Europos fragment" discovered in Syria was once thought to be knitted (Yale University Art Gallery)

The sock seen here was knitted with white and indigo cotton (George Washington Textile Museum)

Current thinking on the origins of knitting suggest that it was developed after 500 CE. Evidence of true knitting (two needles that produce an interconnected fabric made with loops) can be seen in socks recovered from Egypt, dating back to 1000 CE or so. Known as "Coptic Socks", they were knitted toe-up in stockinette stitch, employed complicated colour work and shaping, and often featured Kufic writing and symbols meant to ward off evil. When you consider the complexity of the designs, knitting may have been practiced many years prior 1000 CE.

Want further proof that knitting originated from the Middle East? Knitters work their stitches from right to left, just like Arabic words and sentences are written and read from right to left.

You can knit up a pair of these medieval socks if you like! A quick Ravelry search produces several examples from knitters who have taken the time to painstakingly recreate the patterns and charts for these beautiful Egyptian artifacts.

FUN FACT: The earliest bits of knitting found in Egypt were made with cotton, yes, cotton! This natural material decomposes easily, which is one of the reasons why the history of knitting is not easy to accurately piece together. Wool did not join the party until much later.

The History of Knitting

"Walk like an Egyptian . . ."

How About Those Funny "Knitted" Socks From Egypt?

Socks created using nalbinding, circa 300–450 CE. (David Jackson)

FUN FACT: These Romano-Egyptian socks were excavated from the burial grounds of ancient Oxyrhynchus, a Greek colony on the Nile in Central Egypt and given to the Victoria and Albert Museum in 1900 by Robert Taylor Esq., "Kytes", Watford.

At one time mistaken for knitting, just like the Dura Europos fragment we just looked at, it's now understood that these unusual socks were actually made using a nalbinding technique sometime in the 4th to 5th century. Currently housed at the Victoria and Albert Museum in London, they were excavated from ancient Greek burial grounds in Egypt at the end of the 19th century and represent one of the most famous examples of textile-making we have today.

They have a divided toe and it's thought that they were meant to be worn with sandals, which proves that the wholly unfashionable "socks and sandals" phenomenon goes back at least that far … rest assured, it's not just your dad!

In fact, it's closer to sewing than knitting, but many believe this single-needle method was a forerunner to knitting with two needles. It makes sense because just like knitting, nalbinding uses a single thread to produce a stretchy fabric. One big difference though is that one must employ a limited length of yarn when nalbinding because the yarn is worked right through the loop. Nalbinding needles are generally large, blunt and flat. With somewhat of an oblong shape, they have an eye on a wider middle or end for threading.

Diagram of a nalbinding needle

The History of Knitting

"When you are knitting socks and sweaters and scarves, you aren't just knitting. You are assigning a value to human effort. You are holding back time. You are preserving the simple unchanging act of handwork."

Stephanie Pearl-McPhee

Discovery of the Oldest Ball of Yarn

You might think that you have the oldest ball of yarn in your stash but I bet it's nowhere close to being 3,000 years old!

In July of 2016, a 3,000-year-old ball of yarn was discovered at Must Farm, an archaeological site currently being excavated by the Cambridge Archaeological Unit with support from the University of Cambridge. This incredible Bronze Age settlement is located near Peterborough, in Cambridgeshire, England.

At only a couple centimetres in size, it's astonishing to imagine that such a tiny and fragile artifact was able to survive in the sediments for over three millennia!

1 cm

Discovered at Must Farm, July 2016 (Must Farm Archaeology)

FUN FACT: At the same time that this tiny ball of yarn was discovered, also excavated was a small bobbin with thread wrapped around it and still intact!

NOTE:
For purists reading this, this discovery is technically thread, likely used for a sewing-like technique, as opposed to knitting. It should be noted that thread is categorised as a type of yarn which is twisted ply, and that this book uses the terms interchangeably.

The History of Knitting

"Knitting never was 'just for grandmas'..."

Bros and Rows: When Men Ruled the Knitting Guilds

Around the 11th century or so, knitting made its way to Europe through Spain by way of the Arabs – either during the Islamic Conquest or brought back by Spaniards during the Crusades. Recovered artifacts from this era show that the Catholic Church was fond of using knitting to create liturgical items like silk pillows.

By the 14th century, knitting could be found everywhere in Europe and men were knitting up a storm. Knitting guilds began to be established in France and these professional institutions would spread throughout the land over the next two centuries or so. Essentially labour unions as we know them today, knitting guilds ruled what had now become a highly-skilled, professional trade. In the United Kingdom in the 1500s, it was Queen Elizabeth I who advocated for the creation of knitting guilds. A fan of the popular fashion trend, she was known to include knitted stockings and sleeves in her gown ensembles. Her father,

Henry VIII, was fond of wearing knitted stockings. (The term "worsted" is derived from the town of Worstead, England, a manufacturing centre for yarns and cloth during 1250–1300.)

FUN FACT: According to knitting historian Richard Rutt, the purl stitch, a stitch commonly used to create stockinette fabric when knitting flat, is a late invention. The earliest datable purl stitches are on the stockings of Eleonora of Toledo, a Spanish noblewoman who was Duchess of Florence in the 1500s.

So back to the guilds … young men who wanted to become master hand-knitters would have to leave their families to take live-in apprenticeships. It took about six years to learn the skill and the trade.

Then in 1589 it all came crashing down when an English clergyman and inventor named William Lee invented the stocking frame, a mechanical knitting machine which imitated the movements of hand knitters. His invention represented the first major foray into the mechanisation of the textile industry and was later understood to have played an early role in the Industrial Revolution. This marked the beginning of the end of men's sovereignty over hand-knitting …

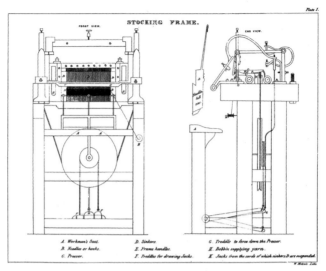

Plate I.

STOCKING FRAME.

FRONT VIEW.   END VIEW.

A. Workman's Seat.   D. Sinkers.   G. Treddle to force down the Presser.
B. Needles or hooks.   E. Frame handles.   H. Bobbin supplying yarn.
C. Presser.   F. Treddle for drawing Jacks.   K. Jacks from the cords of which sinkers D are suspended.

W. Monais Lith.

Lee's Knitting Frame

FUN FACT: Although men dominated hand-knitting during this era, it was around the 14th century that we began to see examples of women knitting, mostly upper-class women. In this famous painting, "Visit of the Angel, from the Right Wing of the Buxtehude Altar" by Master Bertram of Minden, we see Mary, the mother of Jesus, knitting with four needles in the round. Known as the Knitting Madonnas, there were several famous depictions of Mary knitting next to the baby Jesus.

And along came Mary ...

Tricoteuses: Knitting and the French Revolution

The Women's March on Versailles is understood to be one of the earliest and most significant events of the French Revolution and funny enough, it leads to knitting … as you may have guessed!

On the morning of 5 October 1789, female vendors from the marketplaces of Paris began rioting over the high price and scarcity of bread. Their demonstrations became entwined with those of other political agitators – namely revolutionaries who were fighting for liberal political reforms and a constitutional monarchy for France. Eventually the group of market women and their allies grew into the thousands. After looting the armoury for weapons, they marched to the Palace of Versailles, besieged the palace and successfully voiced their demands to King Louis XVI. They were successful and the King and his family returned with them to Paris the next day.

The market women quickly became recognised as heroines and their status was elevated among the working classes. This caused the revolutionary government to begin to worry about the women's power and they eventually forbade them from forming political groups. When the government eventually refused to let the women take their usual seats in the gallery, the women assembled themselves by the guillotine at the square called Place de la Révolution.

Louis XVI

It was here they would watch the executions, knit and act boisterously. This behaviour would draw large crowds and some historians believe these market women were being paid to encourage such behaviour. Because of their knitting, the women became known as "les tricoteuses de la Guillotine" from the word *tricoter*, which means to knit in French.

Decades later, English writer Charles Dickens talked about the tricoteuses in his famous novel, *Tale of Two Cities*. He stretched the truth to claim that the tricoteuses would count the guillotined heads without pausing from their knitting and that they stitched the names of those guillotined into their work. This is very likely not true.

What they did do, however, was knit hundreds of red Phrygian caps or "Liberty Caps" which came to famously symbolise the French Revolution.

The History of Knitting

*"Our boys need sox,
knit your bit."*

Quote from American propaganda poster, 1918

Knit for Victory – Knitting and World Wars I and II

The Great War began in 1914 and from the earliest days, women were asked to contribute to the war effort with their knitting. Led by Queen Mary in the UK, the London Needlework Guild (affectionately dubbed "Queen Mary's Needlework Guild") was tasked by Lord Kitchener with the mission of providing 30,000 pairs of socks to soldiers on the front lines.

They accomplished that and so much more. During the war, Queen Mary and her guild knitted and sewed thousands of items for soldiers, hospital patients and others in need. Lord Kitchener even did his part too. In fact, the "Kitchener stitch", a method of seamless grafting that joins two sets of stitches still on the needle, was devised by him and is still used today!

When the United States declared war on Germany in April 1917, its government put out a call for knitted socks, sweaters, wristlets, mufflers and other woollen garments. Guided by the American Red Cross, thousands of volunteers knitted hundreds of thousands of items to go towards the war effort.

Wool socks were especially important for all soldiers during the Great War. The natural wicking ability of the wool fabric helped soldiers stay dry and avoid contracting "trench foot", a terrible ailment made worse by cold and wet trench warfare conditions. Soldiers often wore two pairs of thick socks, increasing the need for more and more socks!

In the late 1930s, the advent of World War II had thousands of knitters, young and old, boys and girls, picking up the needles once again.

Less experienced knitters made simple squares to be sewn into blankets. Scarves and bandages were also an easy way for a beginner to contribute to the effort.

Also needed were socks, gloves, jumpers, fingerless mitts, wristlets, helmet liners and more and, once again, the Red Cross led the efforts. Everyone was encouraged to "Knit Your Bit" and donate warm knitted items to their local Red Cross stations. Yarn brands such as Sirdar, Monarch, Patons and

The Spool Cotton Company published pattern books to support the massive effort. It can't be stressed enough that in allied countries, everyone knitted something for the cause. The Canadian Red Cross estimates that 750,000 volunteers knitted 50 million articles during World War II.

American Red Cross Poster, 1918

New York City WPA War Service, 1942 (Smithsonian)

FUN FACT: It was during World War II that continental knitting, a style of knitting associated with Germany, became less popular. Knitters adopted the English style, the difference being that one held the yarn with the right hand instead of the left. In recent years, continental knitting has gathered many advocates and it's not surprising given it's a more efficient way to knit!

The "Knit Your Bit" programme is still in operation today. Through the American Red Cross, veterans of the US Armed Forces who find themselves in need receive handmade hats, scarves and other winter clothing items.

Another interesting titbit to note, during World War II people were barred from mailing knitting patterns abroad for fear they contained coded messages. The Office of Censorship was concerned because at one time the Belgian resistance had recruited old ladies who lived by railway yards to monitor and record the comings and goings of trains in their knitting.

Pattern examples from the *Knit For Victory* pattern book from The Spool Cotton Company, 1943

HONOURABLE MENTION: Keeping the spirit of sock knitting alive today is one Canadian man in Cole Harbour, Nova Scotia. Blake Harris knits socks on a replica sock-knitting machine that was popularised during the First and Second World Wars, "The Gearhart". Developed in the 1800s, this was the machine that the Red Cross gave to families for war effort knitting, along with 10 pounds of wool. Harris calls his company Socks Made on 88, a nod to the fact that he works on the 88th reproduction of a 1924 Gearhart machine.

The Secret Life of Molly Rinker

Knitting and war have a long history that goes
way back, even further back than the onset of
World War I and World War II. One fascinating
tale takes place during the American Revolution
when a secret informant named Molly Rinker used
knitting in public as her cover! This lady spy would
knit socks, looking as innocent as can be, while
passing secrets to rebels, who would then take her
intelligence directly to General George Washington
himself!

To the general public this sock-knitting operative,
affectionately known as "Mom" Rinker, was
simply a tavern owner and operator in the city of
Philadelphia. During the period that Washington
and his troops were stationed in the area, about six
weeks in the autumn of 1777, Rinker was serving
ale to the British soldiers who came to her pub. The
combination of lips loosened by alcohol and her
strong observation skills, Rinker was able to gather

FUN FACT: Next time you're in Philadelphia, you can
visit "Mom Rinker's Rock" in Fairmount Park, located
on the eastern side along the Wissahickon Creek.

valuable information for the American patriots. She would take her newfound knowledge to the highest cliffs of the Wissahickon Valley, where she could observe the movements of the British troops and innocently knit socks … or so it looked. Every so often, she would "lose" a ball of yarn which would later be retrieved by one of Washington's men. Deep within the balls of yarn were secret messages on bits of paper detailing what she had observed and learned of the British troops' operations.

As confirmed by General John Armstrong, who served under Washington, Rinker's assistance helped the rebels at the Battle of Germantown on 4 October 1777, but they did not win. As the saying goes, the British may have won that battle, but ultimately they would not win the war.

On the following two pages is a sock pattern from the era, one that Molly Rinker may have used for knitting her own stealthy socks!

"Directions for Knitting Socks" from the United States Sanitary Commission Bulletin, Volume I, Number 31, February 1, 1865, p. 963

1 lb. Yarn knits three pair socks

Use No. 13 needles (UK 00, metric 9.0 mm), and three-threaded yarn.

For small sock, set up 65 stitches – foot 10 inches long.

For medium sock, set up 70 stitches – foot 11 inches long.

For very large sock, set up 75 stitches – foot 12 inches long.

Leg – Cast on stitches. Rib 3½ inches. Knit plain 6½ inches, keeping one stitch seam.

Heel – Take half the stitches on one needle for the back of heel. Knit three inches, seaming every other row. Then turn the heel thus: Knit three-quarters of your stitches, and slip and bind the first stitch of the last quarter. Turn and seam back, repeating the same on the first stitch of the quarter at the other end, and so on, back and forward, till the two end quarters are used up.

Instep – Divide the remaining stitches on two needles, and pick up on each needle the stitches on that side of the heel. With these and the stitches on the instep needles begin the foot. Narrow at the last stitch but two on the side needles, near the instep needles. Do this every other round until you have reduced the number of stitches on each heel needle to half that on the instep needles.

Foot – Knit on plain till your foot is the right length, allowing 2½ inches for the toe.

Toe – Knit one round, narrowing every seventh stitch. Then knit six rows plain. Knit one round narrowing every sixth stitch. Five rows plain, and so on till you narrow every other stitch. Cast off.

Run heels and toes.

To avoid running, and make heel double, follow directions for heel as above; but on seam needles, slip every other stitch.

(Special thanks to the Atlantic Guard Soldiers' Aid Society for digitising and sharing this historical pattern.)

Knitting and War Today – Making Poppies To Remember

Chelsea Poppies (Lythlady)

November 11th marks the day that World War I ended and in Great Britain, and many commonwealth countries, the day is commemorated by wearing a poppy. This is due to the fact that the red flowers grew in Flanders, a place where many battles occurred. In fact, the area is memorialised in the famous poem *In Flanders Fields*, written by Canadian physician Lieutenant-Colonel John McCrae in 1915.

Knitters have taken up the red poppy as a symbol of remembrance as well. Every year around the globe, knitting groups, legions and auxillaries put out the call for knitted poppies in anticipation of Remembrance Day.

In the UK, the Royal British Legion raises money through the "Poppy Appeal", organising volunteer knitters who make sparkly, triple layered, and supersize poppies to meet the public's demand. One year, one knitter made 600 poppies herself!

The History of Knitting

"And in the act of making things, just by living their daily lives, they also make history."

Anne Bartlett

Making History – The Pussy Hat Project

Co-founded by Krista Suh and Jayna Zweima, The Pussy Hat Project launched in the United States on Thanksgiving weekend in 2016. In response to the unexpected election of Donald Trump as President of the United States and the fear that his administration would not take women's rights seriously, the project mobilised to provide activists planning to attend a Women's March in Washington, DC with a means to make a strong visual statement. For people who could not be physically present on the National Mall that day, the hats also gave them a way to represent themselves and support women's rights. The goal was to activate enough volunteers to knit 1.7 million pink "pussy" hats, which essentially look like beanies with cat ears.

The Pussy Hat Project also inspired many other activists to design hats for both the Science and the Climate Marches which took place in April of the same year. Kristen McDonnell of Studio Knit created an amazing brain hat which really looks like a brain, Joan Rowe designed the easy-to-knit Science March Ocean Beanie, biochemist Rebecca Roush Brown blew everyone away with her ChemKnits project and its GENEie collection of DNA-inspired patterns, while Stanford microbiologist Heidi Arjes created the popular Resistor Hat and Headband. If you like, you can find all of these designs and patterns on Ravelry.

The 2017 Women's March may be over now, but women's rights never go out of style! Show your support and make your own Pussy Hat with this beginner pattern that anyone can master.

EASY PUSSY HAT PATTERN

Materials:

bulky-weight yarn,

Size 13 (UK 00, metric 9.0 mm) 16-inch circular needles

Pattern:

Cast on 40 stitches. (size up or down using multiples of 4 stitches)

K2, P2 in the round until piece reaches 8 inches (approx. 24 rows)

Bind off and seam the top.

Weave in your ends.

Voila, a fierce hat with cat ears!

FUN FACT: The Pussy Hat movement made such an impact on American culture that 'Time Magazine' featured an iconic pink hat on the cover of their 6 February 2017 issue with the headline, "The Resistance Rises: How a March Becomes a Movement." Another prominent magazine, The 'New Yorker', also featured the hat on the cover of their 6 February issue, depicting a modern-day Rosie the Riveter marching in a pussy hat, illustrated by Abigail Gray Swartz. Then on 12 February 2017, the 'New York Times Magazine' published a cover story, "How a Fractious Women's Movement Came to Lead the Left," written by Amanda Hess.

Magazine covers depicting the Women's Movement

Other Political Movements Using Knitting As A Driving Force For Change

Here is a shortlist of a few other political knitters (and crocheters) who stitch for good:

★ **Wool Against Weapons** – formed in 2012, the group knitted a seven-mile scarf connecting the Aldermaston and Burghfield nuclear weapons plants in the United Kingdom to protest their manufacture. People from all over the globe sent in scarves to launch the project in August of 2016, to coincide with the anniversary of the dropping of the first atomic bomb by the United States in Hiroshima and Nagasaki, Japan.

★ **The Knitting Nannas Against Gas (KNAG)** – formed in 2012, these ladies are knitting to end the unnecessary exploration for unconventional mined gas in Australia's prime agricultural land. Read their "Nannafesto" for a deeper look at their actions and philosophies.

★ Sisters **Margaret** and **Christine Wertheim** are crocheting to bring awareness of the world's rapidly disappearing coral reefs. (More on these two later...)

* The **Hombres Tejedores** from Chile, a group of male knitters who knit in public to challenge gender stereotypes around knitting.

* Other visual artists known for their political fibre work include **Olek, Ben Cuevas, Nathan Vincent, Marianne Joergensen, Bristol Ivy, Betsy Greer, Jess de Wahls** and so many more.

2. Knitting Tools, Fibre and Jargon

"There will always be knitting as long as there are two sticks and string."

Types of Knitting Needles

At their most basic, knitting needles are simply two long sticks with tapered ends. Their mission is simple: hold stitches, protect the knit fabric from unravelling and provide a mechanism for the creation of new stitches.

When selecting needles for a project, there are a variety of factors one must consider:

✰ *Needle gauge* (universally measured by their diameter and always in millimetres) – this is the most important measurement to pay attention to as it determines the size of the stitches – bigger needle = bigger stitches.

✰ *Needle length* – a personal choice in many cases, but you want longer needles for projects with lots of stitches.

☆ *Type of needle* (straight, circular, double-pointed, etc) – largely depends on the project, small socks usually call for circulars or double-pointed needles, while scarves work up really well on straight needles.

☆ *Needle material* – also a personal choice in many cases, but certain materials work better with certain yarns. For example, metal is more slippery than wood and if you're working with a delicate yarn such as mohair, metal might be the better choice since it won't hold the fibres in the same way wood would.

In the past, knitting needles were often made from tortoiseshell, ivory and walrus tusks – materials that would never be used today. Now knitting needles are commonly made from bamboo, titanium, aluminium, steel, wood, plastic, glass, casein and carbon fibres.

Types of Needles

Single-Pointed – very common, always used in pairs; most popular type of needle depicted in pop culture.

FUN FACT 1: Seasoned knitters keep a gauge converter handy because they know that needle sizes are not standardised around the world. For example, in the UK and Canada, thinner needles are indicated by a larger number, whereas in the US the opposite is true. If you're stuck, remember that needles are measured by their diameter and always in millimetres.

Double-Pointed – oldest needles known; used in sets of 4 to 5; commonly used for socks, sleeves and anything tube-like.

Cable – special double-pointed needle used to hold a small number of stitches temporarily; usually called for in cable patterns.

FUN FACT 2: The world's largest single–pointed knitting needles weigh 25 pounds each and stand over 13 feet tall. Made by Jim Bolin, Jeanette Huisinga of the Yarn Studio in Illinois had to knit a 10 x 10 foot square with the needles for them to qualify for the title.

Circular – made of two pointed, straight tips connected by a flexible cable; used for both knitting flat or knitting in the round.

FUN FACT: Although nascent, 3D-printed knitting needles are becoming popular and a quick search for printable 3D models shows several free designs that are now available.

Knitting Tools, Fibre and Jargon

"Knitting is not a hobby, it's a post-apocalyptic life skill."

Ancillary Accessories

Knitting is as much about collecting and acquiring "stuff" as it is about actually producing a garment.

Below is a list of popular knitter's accessories but is by no means everything that's out there!

☆ *Ball Winder* – turns hanks or skeins of yarn into compact centre-pull balls.

☆ *Measuring Tape* – a flexible ruler for measuring project lengths, obviously!

☆ *Needle Gauge* – essential measurement tool to measure needle sizes and project gauge (the general standard is number of rows and stitches per four inches/10.16 centimetres).

☆ *Point Protector* – nerds have pocket protectors, knitters have point protectors … they keep sharp points safe when travelling and they prevent the project from coming off the needles.

☆ *Pom Pom Maker* – every knitter needs to know how to make a pom pom, because of hats!

☆ *Row Counter* – row counting is part of every project, these help keep track.

☆ *Stitch Marker* – used to mark a certain number of stitches, the beginning of a round, where to make a particular stitch and more.

☆ *Stitch Holder* – holds open stitches when not being used by the needles.

☆ *Swift* – holds your hanks or skeins of yarn in place as you wind them into balls, used with a ball winder.

☆ *Yarn Bowl* – often made out of wood or pottery, it's a bowl with a curved, spiral-like slot for holding your yarn in place while knitting. This has become quite popular in the last few years.

Yarn bowl

☆ *Yarn Cutter* – a small, round pendant-like object that houses a protected sharp circular blade for cutting yarn. Inexplicably, many air travellers have reported that this handy little tool often gets confiscated at security checkpoints.

FUN FACT: Lego has increasingly become a building material of choice for looms and ball winders! In January of 2015, French engineer Nicolas Lespour (aka Nico71 – see below) became somewhat of a minor celebrity when he released the blueprints for his fully functioning "Small Mechanical Loom," made 100 per cent from regular and readily available Lego pieces! If you fancy having a go at making this weaving machine, the instructions are still available today.

Knitting Tools, Fibre and Jargon

"Someone told me it takes five sheep to make a sweater. I didn't even know they could knit!"

Natural Fibres – What Animal Produces Which Wool?

Wool, as we know it today, is fairly new.

Timeline:

* 10,000 BCE – sheep are starting to be domesticated for meat, milk (cheese) and their skin (used for clothing).

* 10,000–5,000 BCE – over the next 5,000 years, people realise that some sheep hair is good for spinning so they begin to breed the ones that have more of the spinnable hair.

* 5,000 BCE – Let the spinning begin!

* 4,000 BCE – the people of Babylon are wearing wool clothing and spinning wool on a drop spindle.

* 500–1000 CE – the spinning wheel is invented (it's uncertain whether the invention originated from China or India, there is evidence for both).

* 1200–1400 CE – around this time, the spinning wheel finds its way to Europe.

What exactly is wool?

Generally speaking, wool is a textile fabric made from fleece harvested from sheep. Some other types of wool include cashmere and mohair from goats, qiviut from muskoxen, angora from rabbits, and other types of wool from camelids (e.g. llamas, alpacas and vicuñas).

Alpaca – Alpacas are native to South America and their hair is known for being soft (but more itchy than sheep fleece, so used less often for clothing) and it's often blended with wools like Merino. Different breeds of Alpacas range in five main natural colours (white, fawn, brown, grey and black) with twenty-two different shades, the most of any fibre-producing animal. The rarest type of Alpaca is the Suri which is known for its shiny fleece that hangs from its body in long, twisted strings. Suri fibre is valued for its lustre and softness and is highly sought after by the high fashion world.

Alpaca

Bison – The bison coat offers two different types of fibre, guard hairs which are very coarse and the downy undercoat which is shed annually. The undercoat consists of fine, soft fibres which are quite warm. The bison's coat is appreciated for being soft, warm, water-wicking and hypo-allergenic.

Dog – Yes, you read that correctly. Rapidly becoming a popular trend in America, fibre enthusiasts across the continent are sending their pet dogs' hair and fur into small mills for processing. Called "chiengora" (a neologism that combines the French word for dog, "chien," with the Turkish word for wool from the city of Angora, which of course is still used for wool made from rabbits today), this yarn is inexplicably controversial with many citing they find it in poor taste. It costs about $50 to process a pound of pet fur. Cat lovers don't feel left out – many processors will spin feline fur too.

Goat – An extremely delicate fibre, cashmere is harvested from the undercoat of the cashmere goat. The fibre is quite fine and produces a much sought-after luxury fabric. Incredibly, one goat generally only yields 150 grams of cashmere per year! Couple that with the fact that the finest cashmere comes from the neck region of the undercoat only and you've got one very expensive fibre.

Llama

Llama – Native to Bolivia and Peru, three million llamas currently make their home in Bolivia, making it the main producer of llama fibre and wool, with

Peru coming in second. The llama's undercoat is known to be finer than cashmere, earning its fibre the nickname, "Cashmere of the Andes". Similar to a polar bear's fur, llama fibre is semi-hollow which makes it very warm. However, it is not as popular a fibre as alpaca and is often used locally for rugs, rope and fabric.

Mohair – This silk-like fibre comes from the hair of the Angora goat. Known to be both durable and resilient, it's notable for its lustre and sheen, and is often used in fibre blends to add these qualities to a textile. Mohair takes dye easily.

Mink – Mink hair is short, thick and soft. It's so delicate that once harvested by hand, it's often spun with another stronger fibre to be durable enough to create a garment. A little heavier than lace weight, this is a good fibre for cowls, scarves or shawls. Given the ban on mink in many countries, it should be noted that minks are reportedly not harmed in the harvesting of their hair.

Muskox

Muskox – The fibre produced from Muskoxen is called called *qiviut* and is eight times warmer than wool. It is extremely rare and can sell for $600 a pound when spun! One muskox produces about 6–8 pounds of fleece per year. It's a very soft fibre with no memory, so on its own it's good for garments that have a flow such as scarves and shawls. If you double the ply or combine it with other fibres, you can make other garments such as gloves and jumpers. Production of *quiviut* is rare because there are few animals and they live in remote parts of Canada, Alaska (USA), Greenland, Norway and Russia.

Possum – Popularised in New Zealand in the 1990s, possum fibre is relatively new on the spinning scene. It's a warm, high-performing fibre that doesn't really pill. It's soft to the touch and is naturally water-repellent.

Rabbit – Angora comes from specially bred rabbits raised for their long, fine hair. One of the oldest types of domestic rabbit (the word Angora comes from Turkey) they were later popular pets among French royalty in the 18th century. Angora fibre is known for being very clean (rabbits like to clean themselves) and hollow. It is

Angora rabbit

7–8 times warmer than sheep wool, but one downside is that it sheds … badly. Look for dehaired varieties if this is a concern.

Sheep – Dozens of breeds of sheep make many different kinds of wool, each with their own set of differentiating attributes. A quick internet search turns up over 400 domestic breeds! This is not so surprising when you consider the centuries old practice of domestication. Some popular breeds include: American Cormo, Booroola Merino, Delaine-Merino, Debouillet, Rambouillet, Panama, Blueface Leicester, California Variegated Mutant, Lincoln, Perendale, Romney, Wensleydale and many, many more. In general, there are two types of wool yarn, worsted and woollen. Worsted is spun from long fibres which are smooth, strong and shiny. Woollen is spun from a *rolag*, a roll of fibre created by first carding the fibre, using handcards, and then by gently rolling the fibre off the cards. All wool falls into three main groups: Fine, Long and Down. Fine wools are soft and elastic; long wool is

strong and known for its lustre; down wool is bulky without weight, the most elastic and resilient. The most popular sheep breed in the US is Cormo which have a fine, soft, heavy fleece. Their wool is mostly used for fabrics, hand-knitting yarns, and felts.

FACT: About nine months is all it takes for Merino wool garments to begin to biodegrade! It's considered a fine wool.

FUN FACT: Male shepherds in southwest France would knit on 15 foot stilts – it's true! They travelled on webbed stilts to keep their feet dry while finding dry land for their sheep and to scan the marshlands for any strays.

Yak – Hailing from Nepal, China, Mongolia and Russia, yaks are well adapted to cold and harsh climates. Its fibre is fine, much like the muskox, and is used to make exceptionally warm garments. Despite their large size, yaks only produce a pound of fibre each year called *yak-kulu*, which translates to yak cashmere.

Vicuña – A high-luxury fibre, Incan royalty treasured it and, in the 1500s, King Philip II of Spain was known to love his vicuña blankets. In the 20th century, popular entertainers such as Greta Garbo, Nat King Cole and Marlene Dietrich favoured it. The fibre is popular for its warmth and is one of the finest fibres in the world.

FUN FACT: The Incas believed that the vicuña was the reincarnation of a beautiful maiden who once received a coat made of pure gold in exchange for having relations with an old, ugly king. Widespread belief in this myth made it against the law for anyone to kill a vicuña or wear its fleece, with the exception of Inca royalty.

Five Fast Facts About Wool

1. It's naturally odour-resistant.
2. Wool feels warmer the wetter it gets.
3. It can keep you cool in hot weather.
4. Wool is flame-resistant.
5. Wearing wool makes you fall asleep faster!

Other Animal Fibres Used For Knitting

"The silk moth giveth, the wool moth taketh away."

Silk – A popular fibre among knitters is silk, which is the natural protein excretion of silkworms (and other insects too, but for our purposes here, we'll leave it at silkworms). Silk is an expensive, luxury fibre produced in tiny quantities; pure silk is smooth, hygienic and non-allergenic (the latter point is worth noting since many people have allergies and sensitivities to wool made from animal fibres). It comes in two varieties: domesticated and wild. Domesticated silk is generally retrieved from the *Bombyx mori* moth (rearing silkworms in captivity is known as sericulture), while wild silk comes from the *Antheraea* moth in India. The shiny and shimmering quality of silk comes from its prism-like structure which refracts light at different angles, thus producing varying colours.

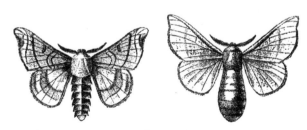

Bombyx mori

Larvae

Cocoon

Pupa

FUN FACT: Silk's discovery is attributed to China's Lady Xi Ling Shi (still widely cherished as "Silkworm Mother"), Emperor Huang Di's 14-year-old bride. According to the Chinese philosopher Confucius, the story goes like this:

One day in 2640 BCE, she was relaxing under a mulberry tree, drinking a cup of tea when a silk cocoon fell into the cup. Clever as she was, the Empress noticed that the fibres of the cocoon unravelled in the hot tea. According to legend, Lady Xi unwound the cocoon and used the yarn to weave cloth. For more than two thousand years after Lady Xi's discovery, the Chinese people kept the secret of silk ... The rest is history, as they say.

Knitting Tools, Fibre and Jargon

"If you had to choose between yarn and your significant other, what's the first thing you would knit?"

Types of Synthetic, Plant-based and Vegan Yarns

Acrylic – Known as the workhorse of the fibre world, acrylic has come a long way from the its squeaky beginnings. Although synthetic, it has a wool-like feel and can be made to mimic other fibres. It is less expensive to produce than many natural fibres, is warm, has longevity, is colourfast, can be washed, is hypo-allergenic and, because of all this, it's used in a wide variety of garments all over the world.

Bamboo – Bamboo yarn is known for being sleek and soft with a beautiful drape. It is derived from the pulp of the bamboo plant and is best used for lightweight garments. It's often blended with cotton or silk. It is considered to be biodegradable, a natural anti-bacterial and it contains ultra-violet protective properties.

Bamboo

Cotton – Cotton wins the popularity contest hands down. It is the fibre most often spun into yarn or thread and its use dates back to prehistoric times. In fact, fragments of cotton fabric dated from 5000 BCE have been found in Mexico.

FUN FACT: It was the invention of the cotton gin by American inventor Eli Whitney in 1793, a machine that quickly and easily separates cotton fibres from

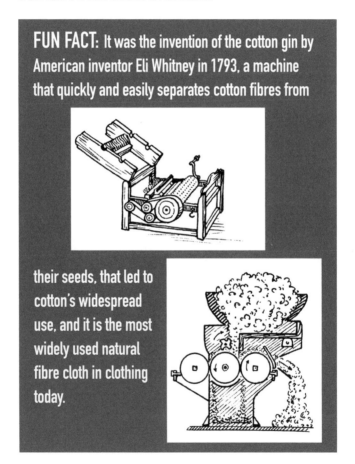

their seeds, that led to cotton's widespread use, and it is the most widely used natural fibre cloth in clothing today.

Hemp – Fast-growing and extremely durable, hemp has been valued by mankind for thousands and thousands of years. The discovery of fragments of hemp fibre can be traced back to 8,000 BCE and in more recent times, Betsy Ross sewed the first American flag with hemp. Traditionally hemp has been used for industrial applications that require strength – ship sails, ropes, etc. It's even been used to make paper. It wasn't until the 1980s that hemp started to enter the clothing market. Hemp holds it shape, is naturally resistant to mould and, like bamboo, it contains ultra-violet protective properties.

Linen (flax) – Linen is derived from the fibres of the flax plant. Dyed fibres recovered from a cave in Georgia suggest wild flax was used for weaving as far back as 36,000 years ago! At one time it was even used for books. Linen is cool to the touch and therefore a popular choice for warm-climate clothing. It has low elasticity and gets softer the more often it is washed.

Lyocell (Tencel) – Lyocell is a fibre derived from eucalyptus trees that are grown on farms and is commercially known as Tencel. It is known for being soft and absorbent. It retains its strength when wet or dry, and it does not wrinkle. It's usually blended with hemp, cotton or wool.

Newspaper – Carried by some specialty yarn shops, newspaper yarn is mostly a DIY homegrown affair with some makers reporting they can "spin" 20 yards of yarn from one sheet of newspaper! Certainly a novelty yarn, as it's limited in its use and delicate to work with, it does present a unique and interesting way to reuse ephemera.

Nylon – Nylon is a plastic that's basically present in everything! Launched in the 1930s, toothbrushes and women's stockings were the first products to feature nylon. As a textile fibre, nylon is usually added to other fibres to add strength and elasticity. Often found in sock yarn blends, it's also sometimes used to help keep the shape of larger garments.

Pakucho – The term "pakucho" means "brown cotton" and we have evidence that this cotton fibre was first spun in Peru over 8,000 years ago. It comes in natural colours, is harvested and separated by hand, and is not grown with any pesticides or chemicals.

Plarn – When you make yarn from plastic bags, you get a wildly useful product called "plarn". A great way to recycle plastic bags from shops, plarn is often used by charities who crochet sleeping mats for homeless folks. It's also great for creating purses, pouches and sturdy market bags, and it's a useful material for yarn bombing since it doesn't degrade.

Rayon – Often mistaken for a synthetic substance, rayon is actually derived from wood pulp. It's processed in the same way as bamboo and it feels soft to the touch. Rayon has no memory so it's not a fibre that keeps it shape, but it can be re-blocked back from the dead. It takes dye well and is known for its nice lustre.

Polyester – The ultimate in squeakiness, this is as synthetic as they come. Despite its bad reputation, polyester is strong, it doesn't shrink, it dries fast, it doesn't wrinkle and it washes easily. It's used in the production of all types of clothing and is often combined with rayon.

Soy Silk / Vegan Cashmere – Touted as a renewable, environmentally-friendly fibre, soy silk is derived from tofu manufacturing waste. It is said to be easy to wash as it doesn't shrink or wrinkle. When worked up, some say it feels like a cross between cotton and linen, others say cashmere. It is moisture absorbent and very colourfast, so it also works well as a raw material for dyeing.

Tarn – Another great way to recycle, "tarn" is yarn derived from recycled t-shirts. It's often used for purses, market bags, jewellery, baskets, bath mats and more.

Emerging Fibres

In the coming years, look for textiles produced from a wide range of unusual materials, including but not limited to:

* milk
* coffee grounds
* kombucha
* wine

* stinging nettles
* coconut
* pineapple leaves
* banana fibre

FUN FACT: People will knit with anything! Some unusual materials have included acrylic paint, dental floss, ramen noodles, computer cables, plastic bags, paper, newspaper, video and cassette tapes, liquorice, glass and more! In 2016, Tamara Orjola made headlines for her environmentally-conscious mission to make "forest wool" from pine needles.

Yarn Colour Variations

There are several different terms that are used to describe yarn variations and colouring:

* *Tweed / Heathered*: yarn with flecks of different colour

* *Ombre*: variegated yarn with darker and lighter shades of a hue

* *Variegated / Multicoloured*: yarn with two or more distinct hues, no pattern

* *Self-striping*: yarn dyed with lengths of colour, automatically creating stripes or patterns

* *Marled*: yarn featuring strands of different-coloured yarn, twisted together.

FUN FACT: Often when you buy yarn, the label will have a "dye lot". This is a number that indicates the batch the yarn was dyed in. For each project, you want to make sure your yarn is from the same dye lot. This ensures your project will be consistent in colour.

Knitting Tools, Fibre and Jargon

"Winter is coming ... knit faster!"

Yarn Weights and the Rise of Mega-Knitting With Jumbo Yarns

When taking up knitting, there are so many variables to know and understand. From needle size to project gauge to yarn weight, a governing body to oversee the standardisation of it all is necessary. The Craft Yarn Council (CYC) does just that and provides invaluable guidelines for all involved in the business of knitting. Based in the United States, this organisation represents the leading yarn companies, accessory manufacturers, magazine and book publishers, and consultants in the yarn industry.

With the advent and subsequent popularisation of arm-knitting around 2013, it was clear that a significant population of crafters wanted to make easy blankets, scarves and cowls and they wanted to make them fast. The internet exploded with how-to content – arm-knitting and mega-knitting on giant needles with hooks became all the rage, while style blogs reported widely on the rise of big-style knitting, fawning over the mammoth-sized blanket one could "knit in four hours or less" …

Yarn makers responded to this popular trend by introducing bigger, fatter and bulkier yarns into the marketplace and in 2015, the Craft Yarn Council added a new yarn weight to its weight standards – jumbo yarn was now *bona fide* and the trend is still going strong today.

Yarn Standards Around the World

Categories of yarn, gauge ranges and recommended needle and hook sizes				
Yarn Weight Symbol & Category Names	0 LACE	1 SUPERFINE	2 FINE	3 LIGHT
Type of Yarns in Category	Fingering 10 count crochet thread	Sock, Fingering, Baby	Sport, Baby	DK, Light Worsted
UK/AUS Ply	1–3 Ply	4 Ply	5 Ply	8 Ply
Knit Gauge Range* in Stockinette Stitch to 4 inches	33–40** sts	27–32 sts	23–26 sts	21–24 sts
Recommended Needle in Metric Size Range	1.5–2.25 mm	2.25–3.25 mm	3.25–3.75 mm	3.75–4.5 mm
Recommended Needle in US Size Range	000 to 1	1 to 3	3 to 5	5 to 7

DK is an acronym for double knit, a term more widely used by UK knitters.

Yarn Weight Symbol & Category Names	4 MEDIUM	5 BULKY	6 SUPER BULKY	7 JUMBO
Type of Yarns in Category	Worsted, Afghan, Aran	Chunky, Craft Rug	Bulky, Roving	Jumbo, Roving
UK/AUS Ply	10–12 Ply	12–14 Ply	14–16 Ply	16 Ply +
Knit Gauge Range* in Stockinette Stitch to 4 inches	16–20 sts	12–15 sts	7–11 sts	6 sts and fewer
Recommended Needle in Metric Size Range	4.5–5.5 mm	5.5–8 mm	8–12.75 mm	12.75 and larger
Recommended Needle in US Size Range	7 to 9	9 to 11	11 to 17	17 and larger

Knitting Tools, Fibre and Jargon

"Knitting is knirvana…"

Making Yarn – Handspun and Yarn Bundles

A quick search on Etsy or Ravelry produces a long list of a wide variety of beautiful, independently handspun yarns. The practice of spinning yarn grows in popularity with each passing year and so does consumer demand, making it a solid career path for the business-minded, and a perfect side hustle for hobbyists and enthusiasts.

Making yarn takes lots of practice and there is a lot of variation throughout the process. This is just one method of many, but generally it happens in these main stages:

1. **Shear the sheep!** This is the true beginning of it all, but most spinners start at the next stage.
2. **Prepare the fleece:** Straight from the animal, fleece can be oily and gross! At this stage, the practice of "skirting" is employed and this is when foreign materials get removed. Things like seeds, thistles and burrs will lower the value and viability of the yarn, so they must go. And, although great for your hands, sheep fleece contains a ton of oily residue. This natural

lanolin should be washed off (or dyeing will be difficult later), along with all the dirt. You want to be gentle with washing as you don't want to destroy or accidentally felt the delicate fleece. To wash the fleece, put it in mesh laundry bags, set in hot water (use a bucket, bath, large sink, etc) and allow to soak with soap for a half hour or so. Agitate the fleece gently with your hands to wash it. Rinse. Repeat. Rinse. Repeat. Rinse. Keep repeating the process until you're satisfied with the results. At this point, you can use the spin cycle of your washing machine to squeeze out any excess water if you like. Lay the fleece out to dry. This last step could take days.

3. **Card it:** Once the fleece is dry, you will work the fleece with a hand carder, a device that looks a little like a pet's hairbrush. The process takes the fibre from fleece to wool.

4. **Spin it:** The next step on the yarn-making journey is to spin the fibre into yarn. Your choices are to use a drop spindle or a spinning wheel.

Drop spindle: This is the easiest and cheapest way to make yarn and anyone can learn to use one. A very portable device, the drop spindle comes in many shapes and sizes. As you spin, the yarn is stored around the longest part of the shaft. The hook at the top is used to secure the yarn to prevent it from slipping as you spin.

Spinning wheel: The spinning wheel mechanises the process of spinning by mounting the spindle horizontally so it can be rotated by a cord encircling a large, hand-driven wheel. Generally, the fibre is held in the left hand and the wheel slowly turned with the right.

Other tools: Not very popular today, a distaff is a staff-like tool you hold under your arm while using a spindle; it can also be mounted as an attachment to a spinning wheel. It's used to hold unspun fibres, keeping them untangled, hopefully easing the spinning process.

FUN FACT: Spinning wheels can be found throughout art and literature, including fairytales such as "Sleeping Beauty" and "Rumplestiltskin". In the French fairytale "The Sleeping Beauty", the princess, is erroneously shown to prick her hand on some part of a spinning wheel in modern illustrations, rather than a spindle.

FUN FACT: Depending on how old you are, you may have heard the term "spinster" used to describe a childless, unmarried woman who's reached middle-age. It's definitely an old-fashioned label, so don't feel bad if you've never heard it used this way ... or at all. Its origins lay in the Middle Ages, a time when a married woman was able to obtain better paying, higher-status work than those who never married. These unmarried ladies would be given undesirable jobs like combing, carding and spinning wool ... the latter responsible for birthing the moniker "spinster".

In those days, it was common for one's profession to be used as a surname of sorts (think Baker, Tanner, Smith, Skinner, Fisher, etc), even in legal documents. Women who spun yarn were given the official title of Spinster. By the 17th century, spinster was being used in legal documents to refer to unmarried women and it kind of just stuck.

THE HISTORY OF THE SPINDLE

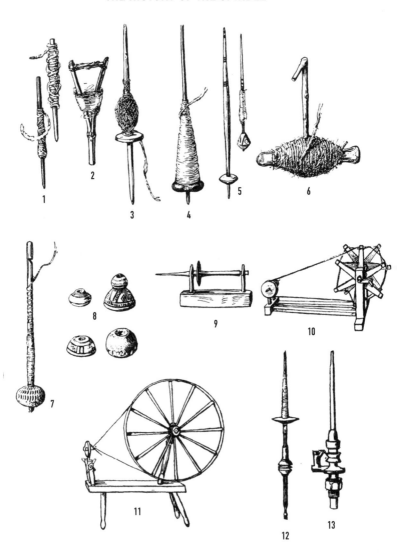

1. *Simple form of spindle*. A wooden peg on which yarn or thread is wound.
2. *Silk winder*. Forked bamboo rod spread for holding wound silk filament. China.
3. *Spindle with whorl*. Shaft of hard wood; whorl of bone; for winding coarse cedar bark. British Columbia.
4. *Central American spindle*. Shaft of palm wood; whorl a hard seed. For spinning cotton yarn.
5. *Peruvian spindle, for fine staple*. The thread is looped over the top of the shaft when the spinner walks along.
6. *Tibetan spindle*. Shaft a twig of cherry, with hook atop; whorl a yak bone. The hook on the spindle shaft enables the spinner to walk about.
7. *Tibetan spindle*. Shaft a twig with notch and groove on the top; whorl of clay at the bottom of the shaft. The spinner walks about.
8. *Primitive spinning wheel*. Spindle whorls of various materials and forms.
9. *Shaft set in bearings*; whorl enlarged for flywheel. The beginning of machine spindles. Finland.
10. *Bobbin winder* in which the spindle is driven by a primitive flywheel. China.
11. Model of large spinning wheel for cotton and wool. Simplest form, without speed pulley.
12. Spindle of small or Saxon spinning wheel, with different sized pulleys to regulate speed. The Saxon wheel works with treadle.
13. Spindle used most generally in cotton-spinning machines in the United States.

Making Sense Of Those Bundles Of Yarn

Hank, skein, ball and cake – you may have heard knitters throw around these terms. Simply put, they are ways to bundle yarn, utilised by both mass-producers of yarn and independent makers alike. Not everyone agrees on the terminology, so take it all with a pinch of salt.

Hank – a hank is a long loop of yarn which looks a bit like a figure of eight. You can't knit directly from a hank, you need to wind it into a ball or cake, either by hand or with a ball winder. This is the preferred bundle for spinners and dyers. It looks cool too and learning to bundle this way is an art form unto itself. Variations include folded hanks and twisted hanks.

Hank

Skein – sometimes used as a catch-all to describe any bundling of yarn, generally a skein is understood to be oblong-shaped with a centre-pull. Centre-pulls are very helpful because they allow the knitter to take yarn from inside the bundle, which prevents the yarn from flopping around all over the place. This is the most common bundling and what you see on the shelves at most mainstream craft and

Skein

yarn shops. Variations include pull skeins and bullet skeins, both sometimes referred to as balls.

Ball – A ball of yarn is what most people conjure up when they think of yarn – the iconic ball of yarn chased by a cat is an image that comes to mind. When you wind yarn by hand you get a ball. Balls are not very practical for storage as they easily roll off shelves. The term ball is also sometimes used to describe a skein – in fact, many manufacturers have adopted this language.

Ball

Cake – A squat cylindrical shape, cakes are what is formed when yarn comes off a ball-winder. They

are centre-pull and many major manufacturers such as Caron are starting to sell their yarns in cakes. It's the best method for showing off beautiful variegated yarns.

Cake

Other Yarn Bundles

Some lesser known (or less common) bundles include cones and doughnuts. Yarn on cones is often used with knitting machines or weaving and contains a large quantity. Doughnuts – more a colloquial than standard term – are similar to cakes, are also centre-pull, but their shape is a tad more flat and round. They often have the manufacturer's label fastened through the centre hole. Other names include doughnut ball and hard-core ball.

And don't forget the hankenskein, sometimes referred to as a "yarn barf", this horrible mess of yarn is what you find yourself up against when things don't go quite right. Maybe you let two balls co-mingle in your stash or maybe you tried to transform a hank into a cake and things went awry … the point is, a hankenskein is pretty hopeless … give up while you still have your sanity!

FUN FACT: Knitting goes in and out of fashion over the centuries. In the 1980s, knitting fell out of favour when an influx of cheap imported knitwear hit the markets and made the cost of buying yarn much more expensive compared to off-the-rack clothing.

Knitting Tools, Fibre and Jargon

"I have OKD (Obsessive Knitting Disorder)… "

Knitting Terms, Slang and Acronyms

Just like any subculture, knitting has its own jargon which includes slang acronyms … lots and lots of acronyms. Technical abbreviations are included in the Knitter's Resources section at the end of this book.

Here's a list of several of the most popular ones:

- Ambistitcherous – the ability to knit in two different styles, e.g., Continental and Combined
- Bicraftual – Someone who does multiple crafts, such as knitting and crochet
- BeauFO – beautiful finished object
- BFL – Blue-Faced Leicester, a breed of sheep
- Bicraftual – someone who knits and crochets
- Bistitchual – someone who can knit English/American and German/Continental (also known as throwing and picking respectively)
- CIP – Crocheting In Public
- Colourway – the name or number assigned by a manufacturer to the colour (or multi-coloured combination) of a yarn

- CPaA or CPaAGG – Completely Pointless and Arbitrary
- CAL – crochet along
- DPN – Double-Pointed Needles
- Dyelot – the number that identifies a particular batch of a colourway
- DS – destash
- EOR – end of row or every other row
- FO – finished object
- Frogging – to undo your work ("rip it, rip it" sounds like a frog)
- Frog pond – area where knitted items are waiting to be frogged
- FSOT – for sale or trade
- FTLOR – For the Love of Ravelry
- GOFO – gorgeous finished object
- HBD – Horizontal Bust Darts, aka short-row bust darts
- HSY – haven't started yet (pronounced "hussy")
- I-Cord – idiot cord
- ITR – in the round
- ISO – in search of
- KAL – knit along
- KIP – knit in public
- KL – knitting loom
- LYS – local yarn store
- LYSO – local yarn shop owner
- MK – machine knit
- Muggle – non-knitter
- OTN – on the needles
- OP – original poster
- OTH – on the hooks
- OPY – other people's yarn

- PHD – projects half done
- PIGS – projects in grocery sacks
- Plarn – plastic yarn
- Pooling – when one colour of a variegated yarn bunches together in a pattern, variations include flashing and puddling (As of 2017, this continues to be a fairly popular trend in knitting. In fact, there are tutorials that teach knitters how to "colour pool" on purpose with different brands of yarn.)
- Procrastiknit – defer all activities except knitting
- Procraftinate – defer all activities except crafting
- Queue – list of patterns or yarns that you hope to make/use one day
- QUIRBLE – queue in Ravelry beyond life expectancy (see SABLE)
- Raglan – a type of sleeve which extends in one piece to the collar and leaves a diagonal seam from underarm to collarbone.
- RAK – random act of kindness
- Raveler – a member of Ravelry
- SABLE – stash acquisition beyond life expectancy
- SEX – stash enhancement experience (buying yarn)
- SAL – spin along
- SIP – sock(s) in progress
- Skank – funny way of saying skein of yarn (skein + hank = skank)
- SSS – Second Sock Syndrome
- Tarn – t-shirt yarn
- Tink – knit spelled backwards, undoing knit stitches by reversing the knitting motion, effectively un-knitting the stitch.

- TOAD – trashed object abandoned in disgust
- UFO – unfinished object
- Vanilla – plain or easy pattern
- WIM – work in mind
- WIP – work in progress
- WPI – wraps per inch (number of times yarn will wrap loosely around ruler in one inch to indicate thickness of yarn)
- Yarn barf – big lump of yarn that comes out of a new ball
- Yarnie – lover of yarn
- YAS – yarn acquisition syndrome
- Yoke – fitted or shaped piece at the shoulders of a garment

FUN FACT: Renowned British-born knitter Elizabeth Zimmerman came up with the name i-cord, which is short for idiot cord. A very simple knit tube (that's why she called it "idiot", i.e. anyone can do it). At one time it was named "stay-lace" and used in corsets.

3. Different Styles and Types of Knitting

"They told me it would be a 15-minute wait, so I knitted you a sweater…"

Knitting Style

Knitting style generally refers to how you hold the yarn in your hand. This covers areas such as the tension you use and whether you're a thrower or a picker. Which one are you?

Throwing Vs. Picking

Also known as English vs. German, and American vs. Continental, there are two main ways to knit. (There are other variations, of course, and we will try to address as many as we can in this book.)

Picking is when one knits with the yarn in the hand opposite the working needle (i.e. the left hand if the knitter is right-handed) and is commonly referred to as Continental knitting, left-hand knitting, German knitting or European knitting. With this style of knitting, the tip of the working needle is used to hook the yarn and bring it forward, i.e. *Picking*. Although hotly debated within the knitting community, it's widely believed that continental knitting is faster because the stitches are formed closer to the needle points and the yarn has a shorter distance to travel. This style of knitting fell out of favour with English-speaking countries in the mid-20th century due to its association with Germany. The movement to bring it back is often credited to Elizabeth Zimmermann, a British-born hand knitting teacher and designer who died in 1999.

Throwing, also known as English knitting or right-hand knitting, is a Western style of knitting in which the yarn to be knitted into the fabric is carried in the right hand.

Despite the names "left-hand knitting" and "right-hand knitting," these knitting styles have nothing to do with whether or not someone is right or left-handed.

The two techniques produce the same fabric, albeit with slight differences. Continental knitters produce stitches that are more square and closer together. Some experts have suggested the difference can be the equivalent of two needle sizes! (Knitters, this is why we must swatch!)

Since World War II, both continental and English knitting can be found in the United States and

England. Japanese knitters tend to be continental knitters and Chinese knitters prefer the English style for the most part. Many other countries are generally known to use continental knitting, such as Portugal, Greece, Turkey, Bolivia, and Peru.

Portuguese Style

In addition to preferring continental style, Portuguese knitters also claim a style all of their own. Sometimes referred to as Turkish Knitting, Incan Knitting, Andean Knitting or Around the Neck Knitting, with Portuguese-style knitting, the yarn is worked from the front so finished stitches look a bit different than English and Continental ones. The working yarn is strung around the knitter's neck or through a pin on the front of the of the knitter's shirt. This method of knitting allows the yarn to be tensioned in a way that it can be wrapped with just one movement of the left thumb, which some claim is easier on their joints; great for those with arthritis and other health issues.

FUN FACT: It is said that crocheters who want to learn how to knit will have an easier time picking up continental style.

One other major benefit to Portuguese knitting is its magical purl stitch. Portuguese purling requires only a small movement of the thumb to wrap the yarn around the needle and is so easy that items worked in the round are sometimes worked inside out so they can be purled 100 per cent.

Different Styles and Types of Knitting

"In a ball of yarn is the potential to make a dream that you have come true."

Melanie Falick

Fair Isle Vs. Intarsia

Fair Isle and Intarsia are both knitting techniques that allow one to knit in more than one colour. That's really the only thing they have in common.

Also known as stranded knitting, in Fair Isle knitting you generally only knit with two colours in one round and when you're knitting, you carry the colour you're not using across the back of the piece. In general, this technique is used when small repeated patterns of colour are called for.

On the other hand, Intarsia is most often employed when the pattern calls for large blocks of colour, like in a picture or mosaic. You don't carry the yarn across the back of the project, instead new colour strands are picked up underneath old ones. It's important to twist correctly, otherwise the piece will remain unjoined.

FUN FACT:

The classic Argyle pattern (seen here) of intercrossing diagonal lines on solid diamonds is knitted using the intarsia technique. The Argyle pattern derives from the tartan of Clan Campbell, of Argyll in western Scotland and from the patterned socks ("tartan hose") worn by Scottish Highlanders since at least the 17th  century. Argyle knitwear became fashionable in the UK and America after World War I, popularised by the fashion company, Pringle of Scotland.

FUN FACT:

In modern times, the term "Fair Isle" has come to refer to any colourwork knitting where the unused colours are stranded across the back of the work — as described on page 94. It should be noted that some people reserve the term "Fair Isle" for the characteristic patterns of the Shetland Islands, especially Fair Isle's namesake, a tiny island in the north of Scotland, that forms part of the Shetland Islands. Proper 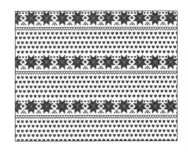 Fair Isle knitting is limited to a palette of five or so colours, uses only two colours per row, and is worked in the round. It gained considerable popularity when the Prince of Wales (later to become Edward VIII) wore Fair Isle tank tops in public in 1921.

Different Styles and Types of Knitting

"It took me years and years of trial efforts to work out that there is absolutely no knitting triumph I can achieve that my husband will think is worth being woken up for."

Stephanie Pearl McPhee

Entrelac, Brioche and Lace

Entrelac

A textured knitting technique, entrelac knitting results in a diamond pattern that resembles basket-woven strips of knitted fabric. It's not woven though, it's actually interconnected squares!

Entrelac knitting

Entrelac allows for colourwork, however, many knitters will choose a variegated yarn instead, creating unique squares of colour using only one yarn.

Another interesting point about entrelac, the finished fabric is sometimes felted to create the illusion of an intarsia Argyle pattern. This happens when the felting flattens the entrelac texture but leaves the different-coloured squares, as if the object were knitted in different colours.

Brioche

Currently experiencing a resurgence in popularity, brioche knitting is a technique that uses tucked stitches, that is, yarn overs that are knitted together with a slipped stitch from the previous row. It produces a fabric with a beautiful, textured honeycomb-like structure. The term brioche itself could be from French slang for "mistake" or it may be a reference to the brioche dinner roll, a bread product formed of two pieces, one stacked atop the other.

Lace

Considered one of the most complex fabrics one can knit, lace knitting is often thought of as a technique for experts. It's characterised by open spaces arranged in such a way to create great aestheic appeal.

FUN FACT: One of the most famous pieces of lace, the Shetland knitted shawl, is so delicate and fine, it can be pulled through a wedding ring! Shetland knitted lace was popular in Victorian England because Queen Victoria loved it and was considered a Shetland lace enthusiast.

Different Styles and Types of Knitting

"Hello, my name is Inigo Montoya, you sat on my knitting, prepare to die."

Double, Illusion and Mathematical Knitting

Double Knitting

Double knitting is a technique that produces a double layer of stockinette stitch fabric with mirror-image colourwork – the trick is that both layers are knitted at the same time! Colour knitting is reversible and shows a negative of the image on the back of the work. It produces a thick fabric ideal for winter accessories.

Sometimes associated with "nerdy knitting", a quick internet search turns up double-knitting projects that celebrate *Star Wars, Harry Potter, Dr. Who* and more.

Illusion

Illusion knitting, also known as shadow knitting, is a popular type of knitting that creates a fabric with a hidden image, viewable only from a certain angle. The effect is created when one alternates rows of two colours so that the raised stitches from one row block out the flat stitches of another row.

The finished work looks like a simple striped pattern from the front, but when viewed from an angle, the "hidden" image appears. In this case, Albert Einstein, designed and knitted by Steve Plummer in 2011, appears when the fabric is viewed from a slight angle.

Albert Einstein – a work of illusion (WoollyMind)

Mathematical

A wide range of mathematical concepts have been used as inspiration in knitting and crochet, here are two of the most popular (i.e. accessible):

* *Möbius band* – Möbius or Möebius, is a surface with only one side and only one boundary. A Möbius strip can be created by taking a paper strip and giving it a half-twist, and then joining the ends of the strip to form a loop. In knitting, there are several techniques one can employ to create a Möbius scarf and it's arguably the most popular mathematical concept to be illustrated through knitting, probably because it is the easiest one to grasp for non-mathematical folks.

* *Hyperbolic surfaces* – although possible to knit, hyperbolic surfaces are mostly crocheted. A hyperbolic surface curves away from itself at every point, unlike its opposite the sphere, which curves in on itself and is closed. Dr. Daina Taimina, a retired maths professor who taught at Cornell University in the USA, is considered a pioneer in this area. Her groundbreaking book,

Hyperbolic example
(Margaret Wertheim)

Crocheting Adventures with Hyperbolic Planes, published in 2009 won the 2012 Euler prize.

FUN FACT:

Speaking of Dr. Taimina and knitting's younger cousin crochet, probably the most famous example of math meeting fibre art is the Coral Reef Project.

An ongoing project and travelling exhibition (Crochet Coral Reef: TOXIC SEAS) by sisters Margaret and Christine Wertheim and the Institute For Figuring, the Coral Reef Project, mixes crocheted yarn with plastic rubbish, combining mathematics, marine biology, feminist art practices and craft to produce large-scale coralline landscapes – think lots of hyperbolic surfaces! The project is a response to the two major calamities facing marine life right now – climate change and plastic rubbish.

The sisters have many collaborators, a core group of worldwide makers and activists called the "Crochet Reefers", dedicated to raising awareness of the issue through their work on this ever-evolving artificial ecology.

Different Styles and Types of Knitting

"Knitting takes balls ... "

Arm Knitting, Finger Knitting and Other Non-Traditional Ways To Knit

Arm Knitting

In 2013, arm knitting stormed the craft world and took centre stage. Dozens of how-to arm knitting videos were trending on YouTube, even mainstream media outlets such as the *Wall Street Journal* were reporting on the new and now popular knitting technique.

Simply put, arm knitting is knitting that's done much the same as regular knitting except that instead of using needles, you use your arms. One of the appealing factors of arm knitting is how quickly one can finish a project – an infinity scarf could be completed over a lunch-hour or weekday commute. The trend was not without it's critics – many long-time knitters complained that the loose-knit gauge looked sloppy and that the technique itself didn't take any skill to do; an affront to those knitters who practised long and hard to perfect their cable game.

Arm-knitting is not as popular today as it once was, taking a backseat to extreme and mega-knitting (giant needles and giant yarn), but every now and again a pattern for a shawl or hammock will pop up.

FUN FACT: As unlikely as it may seem, the emergence of arm-knitting can perhaps be traced back to an Italian performance artist named Andrea Brena. In 2012, the student and aspiring designer presented a project in Berlin called "Knitted Army", in which he used fabric the same length as his arms to create pillows, rugs and more.

Finger Knitting

A great way to introduce knitting to children, finger knitting is similar to French knitting except that instead of a making tube knit with a spool, one makes a flat piece of knitting using their fingers. Some projects you can make using finger knitting include bookmarks, headbands, market bag handles, jewellery, rope and more.

Comb Knitting

Another great way to introduce knitting to children, comb knitting is often used to make scarves and other flat pieces of fabric. It's similar to finger knitting.

Loom Knitting

Knitting looms comes in many shapes and sizes, with the majority being round, square and rectangular. It's also similar to French knitting, except on a larger scale, and projects can be flat or tubular, depending on the project and loom used. The loom frame hosts evenly spaced pegs, which are used to weave yarn around the pegs. A loom knitting tool is used to pull the bottom loops over the top loops.

Different Styles and Types of Knitting

"This weekend's forecast is mostly knitting with a chance of wine."

French Knitting and Knitting Machines

Ask anyone born before 1980 and they'll likely tell you that they did some form of French knitting as a kid. Also known as spool knitting or corking, French knitting produces a long tube of fabric, similar to an i-cord, using a spool and pegs.

French knitting

The spool knitter is known around the world by many different names including, corker, peg knitter, knitting knobby, knitting dolly, knitting mushroom, knitting nancy and bizzy lizzy.

Wondering what use is a knitted tube? Historically, this form of knitting was used to make horse reigns and today you see it used to make mats and rugs, mug cosies, flowers, jewellery, art and more.

Photograph from *Spool Knitting* by Mary A. McCormack, published in 1909 by A. S. Barnes

FUN FACT: The longest piece of French knitting is 31.42 km (19 miles 929 yds) long, made by Edward Hannaford in Sittingbourne, Kent. He has been working on his French knitting since 1989! His hard work paid off and on 12 April 2016, he secured the Guinness World Record for the longest piece of French knitting!

Knitting Machines

Simply expressed, a knitting machine creates knitted fabrics in a semi- or fully-automated fashion. Although fairly accepted today, at one time knitting machines were considered "cheating" and those who used them not "real" knitters. This is rubbish, of course. In fact, those who use them know that knitting machines require great skill, knowledge and technical know-how! There are many different kinds of knitting machines, from the super simple to the highly complicated and computerised. All knitting machine types create knitted fabrics, usually either flat or tubular, and of varying degrees of complexity. Pattern stitches are selected by hand manipulation of the needles, or with push-buttons and dials, mechanical punch cards, or electronic pattern reading devices and computers.

FUN FACT: For a cool $180,000 USD, you could be the proud owner of a Shima Seiki 3D printer, capable of "printing" an on-demand knit sweater in under 45 minutes, including all the finishing! Released in early 2017, the idea for the machine is two-fold — allow the consumer to have a product especially made for them, right on the spot and second, to help retailers cut down on inventory.

4. Around the World in 80 Stitches

"Never underestimate the power of a human with knitting skills… "

Knitting In Peru – The Chullo

Bright colours, textures and bold patterns come alive in textiles from Peru. It's dry climate and effective burial techniques have allowed archeologists to recover many thousands of bits and pieces going back 10,000 years, making it the longest continuous textile record we have. In fact, the Quechua people in the Andes had been experimenting with fibre such as alpaca even before pottery became a thing! It's believed that knitting as we know it today was introduced to the Andes by the Spanish sometime after they arrived in 1526.

You probably have, or have at least seen, the iconic earflap hats from this region. Known as the "chullo", this Andean style of hat is usually

The Chullo

knitted by male villagers and made from vicuña, alpaca, llama or sheep's wool. Just like many knitted garments from around the world, the chullo has its roots in providing protection from the elements, in this case, the Andean Mountain region.

In this region, master knitters, usually men but not always, are known for their extraordinary ability to knit intarsia in the round using needles made of wire or bicycle spokes, either double-pointed or with one end of each needle having a small hook to catch the yarn. Typical fibres for knitting (crochet and weaving too) include yak, alpaca and wool. In recent years, many knitting cooperatives and collectives have formed to help empower Peruvian women and families economically in remote and isolated communities. Often a collective will partner with a non-profit organisation, which operates as a business incubator. The relationship lays a foundation to promote community development through fair trade artisan activities. In other words, groups of local women knitters will partner with a Western non-profit organisation who works with them to sell their knitted and crochet alpaca garments (usually "eco-friendly" is a big selling point) – sweaters, pullovers, ponchos, knitted shirts, jackets and coats, as well as some home textiles – to global markets at fair, living wage prices.

In general, motif patterns and colours on chullos signify regional identity and sometimes marital status.

FUN FACT: Knitwear designer Mary Jane Mucklestone visited Peru to learn more about the country's rich textile history and on the Twist Collective blog she tells the story that while in Machu Pichu she encountered a teenager who had knitted his telephone number into his chullo ... to impress girls, of course!

Around the World in 80 Stitches

"Life's too short to knit with cheap yarn…"

Knitting In The Falkland Islands – Famous Wool

Human population: 2,900
Sheep population: 450,000

Falkland Island sheep

I was fortunate to travel to the
Falkland Islands in 2004 and I
can confirm firsthand that the
islands are loaded with sheep
… so many happy, lucky sheep
living in some of the greenest
conditions on the globe! And it
makes good sense since wool is a major export for
this British overseas territory.

There is a long tradition of raising sheep for
wool on the Falklands – over 160 years! Until the
Falklands Conflict with Argentina in 1982, wool
was the most important income of the island
economy. These days fishing has overtaken wool
as the primary earner, but wool remains one of the
most important and most respected industries.

Everything I saw and have subsequently learned about wool from the Falklands shows a strong commitment to high-quality, cruelty-free wool. Due to the cooler climate, there are no flystrike (myiasis) problems on the islands, which means the practice of mulesing is unnecessary (some would argue it's never necessary). For those not familiar with sheep-rearing practices, mulesing is the removal of strips of wool-bearing skin from around the breech (buttocks) of a sheep. This is done to prevent faeces and urine buildup which can attract flies who then lay eggs in the fleece, causing a myriad of problems and infections for the sheep.

In addition to humane practices, farmers on the Falkland Islands work their farms to organic standards – therefore sheep are not exposed to external chemicals such as fertilisers which means that wool processors will not find any organo-phosphates or other chemical residues in their effluent from these wools.

One important point to make, the term "Falklands wool" is simply a geographic indicator and it does not imply any one breed of sheep or type of wool. Some breeds you'll find on the islands include Corriedale, Romney, Polwarth and Merino.

Around the World in 80 Stitches

"As long as you will have an un-finished knitting project, hope and strength will stay in your family ... "

Knitting In Iceland – Lopi and The Lopapeysa

If you are already four years old
It's time to start working
And for that you need to learn three things
Reading, knitting and spinning.
– Icelandic Poem

It's believed that Icelanders have been knitting since the Middle Ages, or just after. It's part of island life and has been for a long time, a practice so entrenched in the culture that everyone participates – men, women and children alike.

Why is knitting so popular in Iceland? One reason is sheep, lots and lots of sheep. Brought to the island in the 9th century, these long-haired inhabitants have their own distinct genetic pool, in part due to the fact that animal imports to the island are not allowed and have not been for a long time.

Lopi and Five Fast Facts About Icelandic Sheep

1. Icelandic sheep have fleeces that are divided into two layers: an upper layer of long, course hair called the *tog* – think of it as an overcoat that's wet-resistant; and a lower layer called *þel* (pronounced "thel," meaning "underwool") which consists of short, fluffy fibres great for insulation.

2. Before the 1920s, the two layers were separated by hand, but then came the era of *lopi*. *Lopi* is wool made up of the two layers, *tog* and *þel*. The result is a fabric that's light and warm, water-resistant and sturdy too.

3. In terms of colouring, Icelandic sheep (and therefore their wool) are commonly black, white, brown and grey.

4. Because *lopi* is warm and waterproof, it's great for garments meant to be worn outdoors – hats, mittens, scarves, jumpers etc. In fact, the jumpers can be so warm, one will often find Icelanders wearing them with no jacket! That said, it's a bit scratchy, so it's not great close to the skin – you'll want a t-shirt or undergarment underneath.

5. *Lopi* is a magical fibre for three reasons: it felts easily; it is bacteria-resistant (you don't need to wash *lopi* often, but definitely hand-wash when you do); and just like most natural wool – it doesn't burn!

Knitting in Iceland was born of a dark period during Danish rule from the late 14th to the mid-19th century. Known as the "Long Nights" period, two factors contributed to the difficulties – lack of economic opportunities and frequent, devastating weather events such as earthquakes and volcanic eruptions. Throughout this era, everyone knitted all the time. In fact, homes of the era were equipped with knitting rooms designed for the whole family to gather in and knit.

All of the garments that Icelanders wore during this time were knitted: these included jumpers (known as *lopapeysas*), hats, socks, trousers, jackets, underwear, suspenders – even shoes! Knitted fabric was used to create many non-clothing items, from pillows to tents.

Once Iceland gained independence in the 20th century, this evolution gave the country access to

FUN FACT: In 1624, Iceland exported over 72,000 pairs of knitted socks and 12,000 pairs of mittens – whoa! – and not only that, knitters produced four to five pairs of socks per day.

new technologies which impacted the necessity for knitting – it was no longer needed as it once was.

Although knitting never went away completely, hand-knitting had a comeback in 2008, after an economic crisis made it a necessity once again ...

The Lopapeysa

Undoubtedly the most popular garment to be made in Iceland – it's practically a uniform – is the *lopapeysa*, an iconic jumper with a circular yoke and made with Icelandic wool featuring decorative borders around the shoulders. The name is a mashup of *lopi* (the wool we learned about earlier) and *peysa* which means jumper.

The jumper can be zipped, buttoned or whole and you'll find the most traditional designs from companies like the Farmer's Market and The Icelandic Handknitting Association. As of late, this traditional garment is finding new life among young Icelandic designers, so be on the lookout for fresh, updated takes on this classic.

Around the World in 80 Stitches

"Give someone a jumper and they'll be happy for a day; teach them how to knit and they'll be warm and happy for a lifetime!"

Knitting in the UK – The Famous Fisherman's Jumper

The history behind these popular jumpers is layered and complicated, with many stories and myths likely embellished and amplified by one very ambitious yarn shop owner ... so let's try to unravel it all, but please understand that there is no definitive history in this section. Glean what you will and feel free to do your own research and reading on the subject if you are inspired to do so ...

Fishermen's jumper

It all starts with the Gansey (sometimes referred to as a Guernsey), the original fisherman's jumper of the British Isles. Often knitted in navy blue (all in one piece on five or more needles!), these jumpers were actually worn by *bona fide* fishermen. So much of their design is based on necessary technical details such as natural wool knit in a tight gauge to wick the water away, and a double cast-on that provides longevity. Some historians and fibre experts believe that because these patterns were made by mothers, wives and sweethearts who shared their patterns by word-of-mouth only, that regional similarities may account for the popular story that the patterns and particular designs were associated with family lines so that drowned fishermen could more easily be identified … more on that later.

Then there's the Gansey's descendant, the Aran. Believed to have originated from the Aran Isles (three islands off the coast of Ireland called Inishmore, Inishman and Inisheer), Aran-knit jumpers have many of the same features as the Gansey, combining dense cabling, ribbing, a variety of textured stitching and bobbles with drop-shoulder designs.

Traditionally made of wool, which we have already learned has a natural water-wicking property that prevents moisture from being retained in the fabric, Aran sweaters are traditionally a light colour, white or off-white.

Myths and Controversies
It's often repeated that both Ganseys and Arans were

knitted along familial/regional lines to assist in the identification of drowned sailors. It's possible that this is true, especially in the case of the Gansey, but it's also possible that the legend was made up as part of one small yarn shop's marketing outreach. In the case of the Aran in particular, there is not a lot of evidence to support its existence before the 1890s. In fact, the first commercially available Aran jumper patterns didn't appear until the 1940s and it wasn't until 1956 that the first Aran design was featured in *Vogue Knitting*.

Alice Starmore, a professional needle worker and author of the book *Aran Knitting*, agrees that this is all one big myth, fabricated and perpetuated by one Heinz Edgar Kiewe, a yarn shop owner who self-published a book called *The Sacred History of Knitting* in which he claimed, erroneously, that some stitch patterns have a traditional interpretation, often of religious significance.

It's believed that at one point Kiewe noticed similarities between Aran cables and centuries-old Celtic knots carved in stone and concluded that Aran knitting was at least as old. Kiewe's observations have been debunked by many others, including knitting historian Richard Rutt, and Marilyn Roberts, a former editor of McCall's Needlework.

Kiewe, a Prussian-born textile enthusiast who ran a yarn shop called Art Needlework Industries Ltd. in Oxford, England, during the mid-twentieth century, also perpetuated these other wacky myths:

- The moss stitch is said to signify an abundance of growth.

- The blackberry stitch represents nature.

- The honeycomb is a said to be a lucky stitch, signifying plenty.

- Lattice or basket stitches represent the old wicker basket patterns.

- The Ladder of Life and Tree of Life represent the stages of life.

Knitting In The UK: Shetland Islands Sheep

Human population: 22,000
Sheep population: 440,000

Shetland sheep

A popular destination for knitting tourists, the Shetland Isles (or Islands) is a subarctic archipelago situated northeast of the island of Great Britain and forms part of Scotland. Farming in the area is mostly concerned with the raising of Shetland sheep, believed to have originated prior to 1000 AD, and famously known for their spectacularly fine wool. Sheep are so important to the area that in November of 2011, wool produced in the Shetlands gained protected geographical status with a protected designation of origin (PDO) classification of "Native Shetland Wool". It was the first time a non-food product in the UK received this status.

The Shetland sheep is a small breed which is also raised for meat and for conservation grazing. A hardy breed, the Shetland sheep has survived for centuries in harsh conditions. They have retained many of their primitive instincts, which makes them easier to care for than many other domesticated breeds.

FUN FACT: United States President Thomas Jefferson once owned a killer Shetland sheep. Unlike modern Shetlands, Jefferson's ram had four horns. Kept with dozens of other sheep on President's Square in front of the White House, in 1808 it attacked several people cutting across the square, killing a young boy. Eventually the ram was moved to Monticello, Jefferson's private estate in Virginia, where it continued to be violent and was soon put down.

A valuable commodity for centuries now, the fine wool produced by the farmers of the Shetland Islands comes in many shades and is often left undyed. Eleven main colours are recognised by the breed association: light grey, grey, white, emsket (dusky bluish-grey), musket (light greyish-brown), shaela (dark steely-grey), black, fawn, moorit (reddish-brown), mioget (honey-toned, yellowish-brown) and dark brown.

In terms of coat patterns and markings, there are 30 different designations which occur in many combinations. Some of the more humorous names include *katmoget*, which translates to badgerface, and signifies a sheep with a dark belly and dark shading around the nose and eyes, while being lighter elsewhere; and *yuglet*, a light sheep with dark "panda" patches around the eyes.

It should be noted that Tweed is also produced from the coarser Shetland wool, but the Isles are best known for their colourful knitwear (made using the Fair Isle knitting technique you read about earlier) and for the traditional knitted lace shawls which are so delicate and fine, they will pass through a wedding ring.

The Shetland Islands have such a long and wonderful history with sheep, wool and knitting that there are dozens of books on the subject. If you'd like to learn more, I encourage you to explore what's out there.

Around the World in 80 Stitches

"Knitters come with strings attached…"

Knitting In Norway – Selbu Mittens and The Selburose

Norway's love affair with needles and yarn began seriously sometime in the 15th century. Historians speculate that the practice was introduced the century prior by Danish knitters who travelled through Normandy as the oldest retrieved traces of knitted garments found in Norway date back to the 1500s.

The region is best known for its knitted eight-point star-roses pattern from Selbu (a municipality in Norway), commonly referred to as the Selburose. In the shape of a regular octagram, this traditional motif is most often used today for all types of winter clothing, but originated first as a vertical column of two snowflakes on the front side of mittens, today known as "Selbu mittens" or "Selbuvotten".

Selbu mittens

The origin of these mittens is attributed to a young girl named Marit Emstad, who, in 1857 attended church with her two sisters, all wearing what we now know as Selbu mittens, knitted by her. Marit's two-colour, two-strand technique fascinated the community tremendously and was quickly adopted across the land. Today there are over 400 "registered" mitten patterns alone!

FUN FACT: In February of 2014, 90 Norwegian women were recognised by the Guinness World Records for knitting the world's largest pair of mittens – or more precisely, knitting the largest pair of Selbu Mittens! As the mittens were hand-knitted at different times (long story short, the ladies originally tried to set the record with only one mitten, they were told they needed a pair), their dimensions vary slightly: the left mitten measures 2.37 m long (7 ft 9.31 in) and 1 m (3 ft 3.37 in) wide, while the right mitten measures 2.38 m (7 ft 9.7 in) long and 94.8 cm (3 ft 1.32 in) wide.

The Selburose motif and its many variations continue to be the most commonly used, modified and adapted visual in Norwegian knitting. In fact, the traditional motif is recognised outside of the country as a symbol of Norway and Norwegian folk art. When you think of the stereotypical, ready-to-wear ski jumper – such as those worn by Norway's Olympic athletes since 1956 – they often incorporate the Selburose. The Selburose is also present in English knitting terms, sometimes also referred to as a Selbu star or Norwegian star.

Other famous knitwear from Norway include: The traditional *lusekofte* which translates literally to "lice jacket" so named for its black and white diagonal check pattern ... you know it as a cardigan. It's considered to be casual attire and is mostly worn by men.

The *mariusgenser* or marius sweater, Norwegian-style knitted jumper (without lice), often knitted in the colours of the Norwegian flag – red, white and blue.

Around the World in 80 Stitches

"I don't have a knitting problem, I can stop after this row..."

Knitting in Japan – Tabi Socks, Visual Patterns and Amigurumi

Knitting does not play a huge part in Japan's history, but there is no denying that Japan has had a significant impact on knitting and fibre arts around the globe. From minimalist design to popular yarns such as *Noro*, to tiny crochet dolls called *amigurumi*, to visual patterns, let's take a brief look, you may even encounter a knitting samurai or two ...

During the Edo period (1615–1868), Japan purposefully isolated itself from the outside world. There was some trade with the Dutch and Chinese, but very little. It's believed that hand-knitted garments found their way into Japan through this trading with the Dutch. The oldest surviving examples of knitting, used but probably not made in Japan, include seven knitted stockings (three made from silk, and four from cotton) and are on display at the Suifumyotokukai Syokokan museum, in Mito City. These garments were the personal effects of of Mitokomon-Mitukuni Tokugawa (1628–1700), understood to be the first grandson of Ieyasu Tokugawa, the first Shogun of Japan.

After the Edo period, Japan's military structure began to evolve into a more Western hierarchy due to influence from America and this created a climate in which the Samurai class had less influence and was needed less. The new military personnel needed warm gloves, socks and other knitted garments, so many Samurai stepped up to the task to supplement their income with knitting!

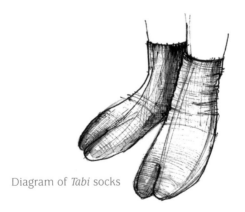

Diagram of *Tabi* socks

Among the garments they knit were *Tabi* a Japanese style of sock, sometimes colloquially referred to as "ninja socks." *Tabi* socks, with their split toes, had long been worn by Samurai, Shinto priests and Kabuki artists because of the added flexibility of movement they provided.

In the later part of the 1800s, missionaries descended upon Japan and began to convert the Japanese people to Christianity. With this brought Christian teachings which included embroidery and knitting. Knitting became a regular part of many schools' teaching curriculum.

> **FUN FACT:** Only cm (m or mm) is used as measurement. Using another measurement system (including inch and yard of the imperial system more commonly used in the USA) is against the law in Japan.

The most powerful influence on modern Japanese knitting was a man from Osaka named Izo Matukawa. After learning to knit from two Christian missionaries in the early 1880s, Matukawa was inspired to devote his life to the study and craft of knitting, including dyeing techniques. It can be argued that the Japanese method of making hand-knitting patterns with charts began with him. He was the first person to adapt knitting patterns visually, a rendering that is still very much part of Japanese knitting culture today. Matukawa led knitting workshops to teach his method and in 1886, he published his own handbook, entitled *Step by Step Knitting Patterns.*

While visual patterns make up a large component of what one thinks of when they think of Japan and knitting, another area is quite significant as well and that's *amigurumi. Amigurumi* is the Japanese art of knitting or crocheting small creatures made of yarn (most commonly crochet). The word itself is a portmanteau of the Japanese words *ami*, meaning crocheted or knitted, and *nuigurumi*, meaning stuffed doll. The tiny crafts had been popular in Japan for several decades before the practice first began appealing to the masses around the globe sometime in 2003. It's thought that *amigurumi* as a term may have originated after World War II, a time when knitted and crochet toys and dolls may have been an alternative for families during the huge economical crisis of the time.

Today *amigurumi* can be found everywhere all around the world. Typically, an *amigurumi* artist will draw inspiration from pop culture – *Harry Potter, Star Wars, Dr. Who, Game of Thrones* and comic book characters are just a few of the popular themes influencing *amigurumi* culture. The trend is so popular that RESOBox, a niche art gallery and restaurant in Queens, New York, hosts a popular World Amigurumi Exhibition every year. Entries to the show flood in from all over the globe.

Another Japanese fibre trend, although not as popular as *amigurumi* at the moment, is worth a mention and that's the art of felting. In 2015, a group of students from the Japan School of Wool Art (they actually have a school specifically for fibre arts!) made giant, wearable, realistic cat heads that captured the attention of mainstream media and fibre enthusiasts. Led by art teacher Housetu Sato, the masks are still influencing crafters today. In fact, in late 2016, the *Daily Mail* predicted that needle-felting will be the next big trend in hobby crafts!

Around the World in 80 Stitches

*"I have sharp sticks and a lot of balls,
be afraid ... very afraid."*

Knitting in New Zealand – Sheep

Human population: 4.4 million
Sheep population: 30 million

Knitting first came to New Zealand through missionary immigrants from Europe, including those from the Shetland Islands. Women were primarily the knitters in the family, but working men were known to knit too. Among the most common items made were baby clothes, socks and shawls.

Just like in other parts of the world, New Zealanders were asked to knit their bit too during World War I, especially socks, facecloths and balaclavas. In

FUN FACT: The Hokitika Sock Machine Museum in the town of Hokitika offers a collection of antique sock-knitting machines and invites visitors to knit their own socks!

August 1916 alone, it's been reported that over 130, 000 items were contributed to the cause, popularising knitting as a major domestic activity, skills that would come in handy for many years to come, especially during the Great Depression, a time when many women would rely on selling their handmade items to put food on the table for their families.

In the 1940s, the world heeded the call for knitting during World War II and New Zealanders stepped up to the task once again, contributing over one million knitted items by May 1945.

After World War II, knitting slowly began to fall out of favour, especially as store-bought clothes became

FUN FACT: The Maori, who arrived in New Zealand about 500 years before the Europeans did, had a unique way of knitting. Without spinning the fleece, the women would roll the shorn wool on their thighs. They would then knit the strands with needles made from fencing wire. Known as "uruahipi", the practice was revived in the late 1960s and renamed kiwicraft.

more available and fashionable. It remained a popular hobby for many (as did spinning and weaving) and even experienced a major revival in the 1970s and early 80s, but was not practised to the degree as it once was.

Sheep

It's impossible to tell the story of knitting in New Zealand without at least mentioning the sheep – so many sheep! First brought to the island in 1773 by the English navigator Captain James Cook, they flourished, peaking in 1982 with a population of over 70 million! Unfortunately, New Zealand is currently experiencing the lowest sheep population since the 1930s and now has about seven sheep for every person, down from 22 per person in 1982.

Around the World in 80 Stitches

"Stitch happens … then you frog."

Knitting in Canada – The Cowichan Sweater

Knitting might not be the first thing you think of when you think of Canada, but wool and knitting are very much part of the culture and traditions of this country.

Take for example, the iconic Cowichan sweater of the Pacific Northwest. Often associated with a 1970s aesthetic, the classic Cowichan sweater is easily recognised for its bold, kitschy designs and over-sized look. If you watched the Coen brothers' classic film, *The Big Lebowski,* you know exactly the look. The Dude (a main character masterfully played by Jeff Bridges) wore what is commonly

Cowichan sweater

referred to today as The Big Lebowski sweater. His was actually a "Westerly" cardigan, a style inspired by the Cowichan and debuted by Pendleton in 1974.

Cowichan Valley is located on southern Vancouver Island in British Columbia, on the west coast of Canada. The Coast Salish people who live there are expert weavers and knitters and have been for many years. Before the European settlers came, the indigenous tribes were weaving blankets and textiles from goat wool, duck and goose down, plant fibres and another mysterious fibre from a small, white, domesticated dog, now extinct, they called "the woolly dog". In fact, some 2,000-year-old spinning whorls and blanket pins have been discovered in the area!

Around 1860, European settlers came to the region with sheep and introduced the local people to two-needle and multiple-needle knitting, which they then combined with their own ancient fibre processing and spinning techniques – soon after the Cowichan sweater was born.

The story of the Cowichan sweater is a fascinating one. A combination of typical knitting construction coupled with ancient universal symbols, the sweaters were once very similar to Fair Isle designs but evolved so much over time that they earned a distinct designation. The incorporation of traditional motifs – fish, deer, whale, eagle – make the sweaters instantly recognisable as a product of the West Coast landscape.

The cherished sweaters – it should be noted that no two sweaters are identical – make perfect heritage gifts. In 1959, Queen Elizabeth II visited the region and was gifted Cowichan sweaters for herself and her husband and children and then in 1981, the Prince and Princess of Wales each received a sweater as an official wedding gift from the province of British Columbia.

Many dignitaries and famous people have been gifted authentic Cowichan sweaters over the years, including American Presidents Harry Truman and Dwight Eisenhower, Canadian Prime Minister John Diefenbaker, singer Bing Crosby, British Prime Minister Harold Wilson, German chancellor Helmut Schmidt and many more.

In March 2012, the federal government of Canada designated the Cowichan sweater as an object of national historic significance. They are a symbol of indigenous and non-indigenous peoples coming together, and a symbol of mixing traditonal and modern.

FUN FACT:

Use the word "tuque" outside of Canada and you're likely to get a puzzled look. The word is French Canadian and it generally means a knitted cap, a common form of headgear for seamen, fishermen, hunters and hipsters. Etymologists believe it comes from an Old Spanish word "toca" for a type of soft, close-fitting cap worn about 500 years ago.

5. Why Do People Knit?

"Knit long and prosper."

Major Health Benefits of Knitting

In 2012, the Mayo clinic studied the neurological effects of certain activities such as knitting and quilting on 1,321 seniors, many of whom were suffering minor mental ailments, either from normal ageing or the early onset of a dementia. The clinic's findings were very encouraging for knitters; reports suggested that those who engaged in crafting activities and other such cognitive exercises were 30–50 per cent less likely to develop diseases such as Alzheimer's. That's great news fellow yarn hoarders, we now have the best excuse to buy more yarn! But in all seriousness, when you consider that 35 million people worldwide currently live with dementia and that the number is expected to triple by 2050, knowing that knitting can help is a crucial development in understanding this dreadful health condition.

Over the years, the health message has resonated strongly within the yarn community. Trade organisations such as The Craft Yarn Council have taken the health message to its members to promote through programmes such as "Stitch Away Stress", and organisations such as Project Knitwell who work to "bring the joy of knitting and its therapeutic benefits to persons facing stressful situations by providing expert instruction and quality materials." Even the mainstream press has taken notice, Jane E. Brody's piece, *The Health Benefits of Knitting*, published in the *New York Times* in January of 2016, has been read by hundreds of thousands, if not millions by now.

The Mayo Clinic is not the only source for information on the health benefits of knitting. A little research online will find you links that go deep into the study and give great information on the subject. To get you started, here is a list of several health benefits and positive side effects of knitting.

25 Ways Knitting Will Make Your Life Better

FUN FACT: According to a study published in "The British Journal of Occupational Therapy" in 2013, of the 3,500 knitters they surveyed who were living with depression, 81 per cent of them reported "feeling happy after knitting."

1. Knitting is known to relieve depression.
2. Studies show it promotes good mental health.
3. It can provide a great way to reduce stress and anxiety, and has been associated with PTSD relief as well.
4. It provides relief in times of grief.
5. Knitting can help beat seasonal affective disorder (SAD).
6. It's a great way to practice mindfulness and meditation.
7. It offers a non-medicinal, feel-good high.
8. It can keep your brain fit and insulate it from damage incurred by ageing.
9. Knitting teaches discipline, empathy and patience.
10. It can help control your appetite – you're likely not munching if you're knitting!
11. It's been known to help relieve insomnia.
12. It can help with chronic pain.
13. Doing it reduces negative thoughts.
14. It can reduce or postpone symptoms of dementia, sometimes up to 30–50 per cent!
15. It will improve your mood.
16. Knitters tend to be organised; it can inspire you to be too.
17. Knitting builds self-esteem, especially when you master a new stitch or technique!
18. It can help avoid cognitive impairment.

19. Knitting has been known to help with the delay of memory loss.
20. It can reduce irritability and help you act nicer towards your friends and family.
21. It will help you maintain strong, dexterous hands.
22. It's great for those in recovery and can help control addictions – quit smoking!
23. It provides an opportunity to practise prayer.
24. It offers an outlet to give to others.
25. Knitting helps you find friends and build community.

HONOURABLE MENTION:

In Waldorf schools, kids learn to knit to help them master fine motor skills. Known as "crossing the midline", knitting helps connect the right and left brains, improving overall coordination.

Why Do People Knit?

"Simple acts of knitting, done mindfully, bring great joy."

Knitting For Charity or Those In Need

Knitting for charity is an extremely popular activity especially after Christmas and during the summer months – the times when most knitters are not frantically knitting holiday gifts for friends and family. From hats knitted for babies born prematurely, to cascading prayer shawls for those suffering through hard times, to "twiddlemuffs" for patients coping with dementia, there is a cause you can knit behind!

Items You Can Knit For Charity

Below is a list of in-demand items needed by many charities worldwide – but please note, it's by no means definitive. If you're interested in knitting for charity, I have provided a list of resources at the back of this book, but your best bet is to start local by asking guilds, hospitals, schools, shelters, nursing homes, churches and yarn shops for guidance on initiatives near you. When you find the charity you would like to knit for, it's also a good rule of thumb to call ahead (or email) to ask whether they are currently accepting donations. Often charities get overwhelmed with donations, so it's good to be sure so that your good intentions don't go to waste!

Blankets and Squares for Blankets

Probably the most widely requested item, blankets are needed by a whole host of charities worldwide – Afghans for Afghans, Project Linus, Warm Up America, and more. You can often donate a whole blanket, or if you're pressed for time, a square will often do (double check the charity's size specifications). Many charities host "seaming parties" throughout the year to put them all together.

Dolls / Stuffed Animals

There is an amazing and utterly fascinating variety of need in this category. Take for example the recent discovery made by doctors in Denmark that premature babies who cradle an octopus toy show improved breathing, heartbeat and oxygen blood levels. Apparently the tentacles remind the babies of their mothers by mimicking the umbilical cord! So now neonatal units all over the world are collecting knitted and crochet octopuses! Many hospitals, shelters, fire departments and other civic organisations need dolls and stuffed animals for the children they service, as they provide some comfort in times of great stress and tragedy. There's also an organisation called "Knitting 4 Peace", and they collect dolls called "Peace Pals" to distribute to children in areas of conflict throughout the world.

Hats, Scarves, Mittens

As the weather turns colder, demand for warm clothing grows. Local shelters and churches often have demand, so be sure to check with them first. You can also knit for the troops, the Scarves For Troops Program in the United States comes to mind as one, but there are many others you'll be able to surface with a quick online search.

Many hospitals also accept hats for newborns. I remember when my son was born, he was given a nice knitted beanie, no doubt made with love by a local area knitter – and for that my family was grateful!

Knitted Knockers / Breast Prosthesis / Knitted Breasts

Relatively new on the charity knitting circuit, "knitted knockers" (other names include woolly boobs, boob beanies, etc.) are handmade breast prosthesis for women who have undergone mastectomies or other procedures to the breast. Women have reported to prefer these over traditional prosthetics which can be expensive and uncomfortable. Amazingly, when made correctly, they take on the shape and feel of a real breast and they can easily be washed.

Knitted breasts are also often used by midwives, health visitors and breastfeeding coaches as an instrument to help new mothers learn more about attachment. Contact local birth centres to find out if knitted breasts are needed in your area.

FUN FACT: Knitters who participate in making knitted knockers have been known to call themselves "Knockerettes"!

Prayer Shawls / Comfort Shawls / Peace Shawls

Traditionally known as prayer shawls, the secular world has embraced the concept too, often opting for a less religious-sounding moniker such as "comfort shawl". Regardless of what you call it, the point is for the shawl maker to stitch good intentions and blessings into the garment. Upon completion, a final blessing is usually offered before the shawl is sent off to the person in need.

The Prayer Shawl Ministry suggests shawls be gifted for: "undergoing medical procedures; as a comfort after a loss or in times of stress; during bereavement; prayer or meditation; commitment or marriage ceremonies; birthing, nursing a baby;

bridal shower or wedding gift; leading ritual;
first menses or croning rites of passage; during
an illness and recovery; ministering to others;
graduation, birthday, anniversary, ordination,
holiday gifts; or just socialising."

It's easy to see why this is such a popular item to
knit.

Slippers
Quick to knit and very practical, slippers are
often needed in hospitals for cancer patients, in
treatment centres, shelters, orphanages and many
other places. Many charity knitters will paint the
bottoms with silicone or fabric paint to make them
safer and non-skid – there are many free tutorials
available online if you would like to have a go.

Twiddle Muffs
Also a relatively new item to the charity knitting
scene, twiddle muffs (also known as a twiddlemuff,
one word) are specifically designed for patients
dealing with dementia or Alzheimer's. At it's most
basic, it is a double thickness hand muff with bits
and bobs (buttons, pom-poms, patches, beads, etc.)
attached inside and out. The idea is that it offers
a healthy stimulation activity for restless hands.
In the UK, an organisation called Knit for Peace
collects and distributes them to hospitals.

Yarn Bombs

Understood to have originated in Texas with Magda Sayeg (Knitta Please) in 2005, yarn bombing has quickly become one of the most popular forms of street art worldwide. From Queen Babs in Australia (aka Jane Balke Andersen), to Olek and London Kaye in New York City, to Knits For Life (Lorna and Jill Watt) and the Yarnbomber in California (Stephen Duneier), to Deadly Knitshade and her Knit The City crew in London, UK (aka Lauren O'Farrell), it makes sense that this collaborative type of art would get mixed up with charitable causes eventually!

Often a collective of yarn bombers will get together and, with permission from their city officials, they'll yarn bomb trees in a park, or benches in a public area, or in the case of KNIT CamBRIDGE (in Ontario, Canada), a whole bridge! The brainchild of Sue Sturdy, the idea was to cover the bridge in knitting to remind locals of their city's textile production and manufacturing heritage. Over a thousand knitters contributed knit (and crochet) pieces and the installation was unveiled to the public on 11 September 2010.

As is the case with most yarn bombing projects of this scale, once the pieces were adored by the masses, they were taken down for cleaning, repurposing and distribution to local charities and shelters.

We'll take a deeper look at the yarn bombing phenomenon in the next section.

FUN FACT:

16,000 cable ties were used to secure all the knitting to the Main Street bridge in the KNIT CamBRIDGE project!

Why Do People Knit?

"Stitch and bitch. There is nothing that a little needling can't fix. "

It's Fun And Social – Stitch 'n Bitch

With names like "stitch and bitch" or "knit and natter" or a dozen other clever names, regular knitting meet-ups are happening all over the world every day and night, in churches, pubs, libraries, living rooms and any spaces you can think of.

The term "stitch and bitch" itself is much older than you may think. It's actually a name that has been around since at least World War II! Then and today, the groups, mainly women, meet to knit, stitch and talk, aka bitch and gossip.

In recent times, the knitting groups have been analysed by scholars as expressions of resistance to major political, social and technological change, which we have certainly seen in 2017, with the election of Donald Trump as President of the United States of America and the fast-growing "pussy hat project" movement discussed earlier in the book.

Ravelry

Boasting over seven million members as of March 2017, Ravelry is the treasured social network for fibre enthusiasts around the world.

Started in May 2007 by husband and wife team Casey and Jessica Forbes, Ravelry is devoted to being a free social networking service that also acts as a personal organisational tool – you can catalogue your projects and link them to the greater pattern database, you can share ideas, share and rate patterns, join groups and forums, network with other knitters, crocheters, spinners, dyers and weavers, keep a record of your yarn stash and so much more!

One of the most popular places to socialise in Ravelry are the forums, and one of the most active boards is "Lazy, Stupid & Godless". Commonly known as LSG for short, you'll find threads on a wide range of topics not related to yarn, from Pokemon Go to tax advice, to entertaining demotivational memes, it's quirky, hilarious and often quite offensive – in other words, totally nourishing and 100 per cent required reading. You have been warned …

Ravelry is also an important resource for small business owners and designers alike. Crafters can sell their patterns or yarns, while small businesses such as local yarn shops can buy banner ads through Ravelry's native ad platform.

Something that makes Ravelry a truly distinct stomping ground for fibre enthusiasts is the nature of its community-edited yarn and pattern database. From the newest to the most obscure, if it's been knitted you'll likely find it within Ravelry.

It's Fun and Social – Knit-Alongs (and Crochet-Alongs too)

At its most basic, a knit-along (or KAL for short) is when a group of people get together and agree to work on the same pattern together. This can happen in person – at yarn shops, in pubs, in private homes, at community centres, in churches, at coffee shops; basically anywhere humans can huddle – or it can be conducted online.

Apart from the obvious social benefits of getting together with people to knit, knit-alongs can help knitters learn a new skill or perfect an old one. When you're choosing a knit-along to participate in (there are zillions!), choose one that will challenge you because you'll be able to get tips and advice from the KAL leader and your fellow KAL participants.

Non-Traditional KALs

One of my favourite kinds of knit-along is the "mystery KAL" (or MKAL). Every week the KAL leader, usually the pattern designer, will reveal a little piece of the pattern to work on, but the knitters usually don't know what they're making until well into the KAL! Some fab designers known to hold mystery KALs include Wooly Wormhead, Lee Meredith and Stephen West.

Another non-traditional type of KAL is the "Stitch N' Pitch" which happens in summertime on baseball fields across the United States mostly, but in other parts of the world too. Fans sit together in a special section of the stadium to work on their crochet, cross-stitch, embroidery, knitting or needlepoint projects and cheer on their favourite team. Often a yarn company will sponsor the event and give out free yarn in promotional goody bags.

Organised by the National NeedleArts Association since 2006, Stitch N' Pitch raises funds and awareness for the Helping Hands Foundation which supports mentoring programmes.

FUN FACT: At the 2010 NY Mets/Florida Marlins Stitch N' Pitch event in Queens, NY, the group officially set a new Guinness World Record for the "Most People Crocheting Simultaneously".

Every so often KALs will unofficially align themselves to a television series, so for example, you might knit a jumper to a season of your favourite show, like one Canadian-led Very Shannon did with the recent reboot of *Gilmore Girls*. And this segues us nicely to the next section of the book, pop culture and knitting – fun!

6. Knitting in Pop Culture Today

"As I get older, I just prefer to knit. "

Tracey Ullman

Celebrities Who Knit

Almost every week there's a story in the press about so-and-so celebrity spotted knitting on set between takes, or knitting on the beach, or at home to relax. Knitting is not just for us regular folk you know!

By no means exhaustive, here is a compilation of celebrities who have been spotted knitting (some are better known to crochet, but I've included them anyway).

A List Of Knitting Celebrities ...

Amanda Seyfried	Ann Sheridan
Amber Valletta	Annette Funicello
Amy Adams	Annette O' Toole
Angela Lansbury	Annie Lennox
Angela Merkel	Anthony Anderson
Anjelica Huston	Ashlee Simpson

Ashley Olsen
Ashton Kutcher
Ava Gardner
Barbara Bel Geddes
Barbara Hutton
BD Wong
Benedict Cumberbatch
Bette Davis
Betty Grable
Betty White
Blake Lively
Blossom Rock
Buster Keaton
Cameron Diaz
Carole Lombard
Carolyn Jones
Cary Grant
Catherine Deneuve
Catherine, Duchess of
Cambridge
Catherine Zeta-Jones
Charles Manson
Christina Hendricks
Christopher Walken
Constance Towers
Courteney Cox
Daisy Ridley
Dakota Fanning
Dame Elizabeth Taylor

Dana Wynter
Daryl Hannah
David Arquette
Debbie Reynolds
Debby Boone
Debra Messing
Diane Lane
Doris Day
Drew Barrymore
Eleanor Parker
Eleanor Roosevelt
Elisabeth Moss
Ellen Pompeo
Ernie Hudson
Estelle Getty
Estelle Parsons
Felicity Huffman
Frank Sinatra
Franklin Roosevelt
Gary Cooper
Geena Davis
Gene Tierney
George Lucas
Geri Halliwell
Gina Lollobrigida
Ginger Rogers
Gloria Stuart
Goldie Hawn
Grace Coolidge

Grace Kelly
Greer Garson
Guo Xiaodong
Gwyneth Paltrow
Hal Sparks
Hannah Simone
Helen Hayes
Helen Hunt
Hilary Benn
Ida Lupino
Iman
Ingrid Bergman
Irene Dunne
Isaac Mizrahi
Jane Birkin
Jane Powell
Jayne Mansfield
Jean Stapleton
Jennifer Aniston
Jennifer Lawrence
Jessica Simpson
Joan Crawford
Joanne Woodward
John C. Reilly
John Glover
Josephine Baker
Josh Bennett
Josh Duhamel
Joyce Grenfell

Judy Garland
Judy Greer
Julia Louis-Dreyfus
Julia Roberts
Julianne Moore
Justine Bateman
Karen Allen
Kat Dennings
Kate Hudson
Kate Moss
Kate Nash
Kate Winslet
Katey Sagal
Katharine Hepburn
Katherine Heigl
Kenny Johnson
Kimberly Stewart
Kirtsy Hume
Kristen Stewart
Kristin Davis
Kurt Cobain
Lara Stone
Laura Leighton
Lauren Bacall
Lauren Conrad
Lily Allen
Linda Ronstadt
Lisa Edelstein
Lisa Kudrow

Lisa Scott Lee
Lorde
Louis CK
Louis Lumière
Lucille Ball
Lucrezia Bori
Madonna
Mama Cass
Margaret Atwood
Margaret Hamilton
Marilyn Monroe
Mariska Hargitay
Martha Stewart
Mary Boland
Mary Pickford
Meryl Streep
Mischa Barton
Myrna Loy
Nancy Rogers (Mr. Rogers' mom, she made all his famous sweaters)
Natasha Richardson
Nicole Kidman
Oliver Proudlock
Omarosa Manigault
Pat Crowley
Patricia Arquette
Sir Patrick Stewart
Sojourner Truth

Paul Rudd
Paula Raymond
Paulina Porizkova
Pedro Almodóvar
Penny Smith
Phyllis Diller
Pink
Queen Elizabeth II
Queen Victoria
Richard Rutt, Bishop of Leicester
Ringo Starr
Rita Hayworth
Robin Williams
Rosalind Russell
Rosie Perez
Russell Crowe
Ruth Bader Ginsburg
Ryan Gosling
Ryan Reynolds
Sandra Bullock
Sarah Jessica Parker
Scarlett Johansson
Sean Kanan
Shelley Winters
Shirley Temple
Sienna Miller
Sigourney Weaver
Simon Cowell

Sophia Loren
Sufjan Stevens
Susan Hayward
Sylvester Stallone
Tim Daly
Tom Hanks
Tom Mitchell
Tori Spelling
Tracey Ullman

Tyne Daly
Uma Thurman
Vanessa Redgrave
Vanna White
Viola Davis
Vivien Leigh
Wil Wheaton
Zooey Deschanel

FUN FACT: Before he was James Bond, Roger Moore modelled for knitting patterns!

Eddie Redmayne, Oscar winning actor and star of 'Fantastic Beasts and Where to Find Them', 'Theory of Everything', 'Danish Girl' and 'Les Misérables', started his career as the face of knitting pattern company Rowan Yarns.

A List of Knitters Who Are Celebrities

On the flip side, many knitters and crocheters have become well-known through their handiwork! Here is a snapshot of a few popular fibre enthusiasts – I've included some of my favourite artists, teachers and designers – I encourage you to check them all out.

Agata Oleksiak, aka Olek
Alice Starmore

Allison Hoffman, aka Crafty Is Cool
Amy Herzog
Amy R. Singer
Anna Hrachovec (Mochimochi Land)
Anna Zilboorg
Barbara Kingsolver
Ben Cuevas
Bill Davenport
Bristol Ivy
Carol Milne
Caroline Wells Chandler
Casey Jenkins
Cat Bordhi
Cirkus Cirkör
Clara Parkes
Colette Smith
Dan Zondervan, aka Diva Dan
Dave Cole
David Babcock, aka The Knitting Runner
Debbie Bliss
Deborah Jarchow
Donna Druchunas
Dora Ohrenstein
Edie Eckman
Elizabeth Hawes
Elizabeth Zimmermann
Elsebeth Lavold
Eric Rieger, aka HOTTEA
Ernesto Neto

Franklin Habit

Gudrun Johnston

Hannah Busekrus, aka Hanasaurusrex

Inge Jacobsen

J. Curtaz, aka Binding Things

Jaala Spiro

Jane Balke Andersen, aka Queen Babs

Jenny Brown, aka Hi, Jenny Brown

Jessie Hemmons, aka ishknits

Jim Drain

Kaffe Fassett

Katie Freeman

Koos van der Akker

Kristy Glass

Laura Nelkin

Lauren O'Farrell, aka Deadly Knitshade

Lily Chin

Lindsay Obermeyer

London Kaye

Lorilee Beltman

Lorna and Jill Watt, aka Knits For Life

Magda Sayeg

Margaret Hubert

Marly Bird

Martha Stewart

Mary Beth Temple

Mary Jane Mucklestone

Meg Swansen (Elizabeth Zimmerman's daughter)

Michael Sellick, aka Mikey

Nathan Vincent
Nicky Epstein
Nina Dodd
Orly Genger
Patricia Waller
Rohn Strong
Ruth Marshall
Sam Barsky
Shannon Okey
Shanon Schollian
Shira Blumenthal
Sonya Philip
Sophie Digard
Stephanie Pearl-McPhee, aka Yarn Harlot
Stephen Duneier, aka Yarnbomber
Stephen West
Steven Berg
Susanna Bauer
Susie Hewer
Tatyana Yanishevsky
Tinna
Toshiko Horiuchi MacAdam
Tracy Widdess
Trisha Malcolm
Twinkie Chan
Vickie Howell
Xenobia Bailey
Ysolda Teague

FUN FACT: David Babcock, aka The Knitting Runner, holds the Guinness World Record for the longest scarf knitted whilst running a marathon. Measured at 3.70 m (12 ft 1.75 in), the scarf was knitted at the Kansas City Marathon in Kansas City, Missouri, USA, on 19 October 2013.

David was inspired by Susie Hewer, the knitting runner who held this record previously and had broken it three times at the London Marathon. As a show of honour and respect, David ran for the same Alzheimer's Research charity that Susie ran for.

David Babcock ran the New York City marathon in 2014 to raise funds for the New York City chapter of The Alzheimer's Association. He was not permitted to use knitting needles on the course, so he improvised a finger-knitting technique. Not only did he beat his own personal running record that day (3:56), he also finger-knitted the words: "I'll remember for you" into his scarf!

Knitting in Pop Culture Today

"I find your lack of yarn disturbing. "

Knitting In Film, Television, Music and Literature

Knitting shows up in film and television quite often, it's hard to keep up! Here are twenty-five examples for you to hunt down … it's time for a little #KnitFlix and chill …

25 Times Knitting Took Over Film and Television

1. **Bob's Burgers:** Knitting figures prominently in season 2 episode 3, and this episode is the origin of the infamous meme-spawning line,"What up my knitta?"
2. **Slow TV:** National Knitting Night
3. **Louie:** Louis CK practises knitting in season 5, episode 3.
4. **Book of Life:** Anita Sánchez, Manolo's great grandmother, is seen knitting in her wheelchair several times during the film. I highly recommend this animated movie, it's fantastic!
5. **Pingu:** Season 5 features an episode called, "Pingu and the Knitting Machine."
6. **Wallace & Gromit:** Knitting figures prominently throughout this popular series – Gromit is a big knitter! "Knit-O-Matic" is an especially memorable episode.

7. **Pee Wee's Big Adventure:** Although Pee-Wee is not knitting, it's on his mind throughout this infamous scene where he maniacally says, "the mind plays tricks on you. You play tricks back. it's like you're unravelling a big cable knit sweater that someone keeps knitting and knitting and knitting and knitting and knitting and knitting and knitting!"

8. **The Crazies:** In this George Romero horror film, a seemingly sweet grandmother stabs a biohazard trooper with her knitting needle.

9. **Girls:** In season 4, episode 2, Marnie is seen knitting a scarf for Desi while on a video chat with Hannah.

10. **Enough Said:** Julia Louis-Dreyfus is knitting a canary yellow blanket in this romantic comedy that notably features James Gandolfini (*The Sopranos*) and Tavi Gevinson (*Rookie Mag*).

11. **I Love Lucy:** Lucy and Ethel are seen knitting throughout this classic series.

12. **Never Been Kissed:** John C. Reilly knits in this film featuring Drew Barrymore and David Arquette, who are also both knitters in real life!

13. **Sherlock:** Benedict Cumberbatch's Sherlock Holmes is a knitter, a fact that has also spawned many memes!

14. **M*A*S*H:** Both Margaret, played by Loretta Swit, and Hawkeye, played by Alan Ada, can be seen knitting in this famous television series.

15. **The Big Lebowski:** Okay, so no one is knitting in this Coen brothers classic, but the Cowichan sweater "The Dude" wears is almost as famous as the film itself. Rumour has it that it was his own personal sweater!

16. **Yarn:** This 2016 documentary follows the lives and works of several fibre artists, including Olek and Toshiko Horiuchi MacAdam.

17. **The Addams Family:** Morticia Addams is a knitter, in both the television series and the films, knitting three-armed sweaters and three-legged baby clothes.

18. **Coraline:** A fantastic 3D stop-motion dark fantasy film based on Neil Gaiman's novel of the same name, Coraline wears tiny hand-knitted garments all masterfully constructed by Althea Crome. You definitely want to seek her out, she shares her process in several short films – it's fascinating to say the least!

19. **Clangers:** A beloved stop-motion animated children's television series created in Britain in the 1960s, The Clangers are a family of pink creatures who they themselves are actually knitted. The programme was rebooted in 2015 for an American audience, with William Shatner as narrator.

20. **The Virgin Suicides:** Kirsten Dunst's character Lux Lisbon is seen knitting something purple and pink striped.

21. **Wizard of Oz:** At the beginning of the film, when Dorothy is being transported inside the tornado, she sees a woman calmly knitting while seated in a rocking chair.

22. **Golden Girls:** Legend has it that in between takes, Estelle Getty knitted the sweaters her character Sophia Petrillo wears on the show. In one scene, Sophia is famously knitting a bottle cosy for the sherry she secretly takes to the park!

23. **HitchHikers Guide to the Galaxy:** The Heart of Gold crew turn into knitted dolls during the Infinite Improbability Drive sequence. Bonus: If you observe Towel Day on 25 May, try something new and knit one this year! Have no idea what I'm talking about? The answer is 42.

24. **Orange is the New Black:** For season one of the ladies-only prison drama, Daya is featured on promotional materials knitting a blue scarf using pencils for knitting needles! You'll find knitting and crochet represented throughout the series.

25. **Close-Knit:** Released in 2017, this Japanese film recently received the Panorama Audience Award at the prestigious Berlin Film Festival. Directed by Ogigami Naoko, it follows the story of a transgender woman who becomes a mother figure to a neglected young girl. Knitting is featured prominently throughout the

film – so much so that the premiere featured knitted and crocheted movie posters!

HONOURABLE MENTIONS:

Nastassja Kinski in Wim Wenders' film, "Paris, Texas" (she wears mohair!), Danny's Apollo 11 sweater in Stanley Kubrick's "The Shining," Mary Tyler Moore's iconic tam toss in "The Mary Tyler Moore Show" opening, and in Judge Dredd, Sylvester Stallone is programmed to knit as part of his rehabilitation.

Famous Sweaters and the Men Who Wore Them

Mr. Rogers

Fred Rogers, the star and creator of the world-famous PBS kids show *Mister Rogers' Neighborhood* was famous for wearing knitted cardigans. At the beginning of each episode, Rogers would visit his wardrobe to select a sweater for the day. You may be wondering what's so special about these sweaters … well, his mother hand-knitted each and every one. Rogers featured the sweaters in one episode, sharing with his viewers that they helped him think of his mother ... bringing truth to the saying that a handmade sweater is a hug you wear all day.

FUN FACT: Mr. Rogers is also the subject of one of the most recognizable yarn bombs ever. Using a size Q hook, his iconic red sweater was crocheted by Pittsburgh, Pennsylvania native Alicia Kachmar and placed on his 10-foot-tall statue!

Bill Cosby

I debated with myself whether or not to include Bill Cosby in this book and decided at least to acknowledge the famous sweaters that he wore on the barrier-breaking sitcom, *The Cosby Show*. Mostly created by Dutch designer Koos van der Akke, those sweaters have inspired blogs, songs and even a single-elimination type tournament in which fans voted for their favourite Cosby sweater – the winner was a red and blue number which featured three competitive track runners across the chest. If you're interested in seeing all 131 sweaters worn by Cosby on the series, visit Buzzfeed for the piece, "All 131 Sweaters Worn By Bill Cosby On *The Cosby Show*."

Grant Lawrence

Do you know about Canada's famous CBC sweater? The story goes that in 2009 or so, a well-loved broadcaster (and former vocalist for the band The Smugglers) named Grant Lawrence was approached by a fan for his measurements – she happened to be involved with a clothing company called Granted (the name is a coincidence) and she wanted to knit him a Cowichan-inspired CBC-branded sweater. Today that sweater is something of a legend! It's been hopelessly lost and miraculously found, travelled to at least nine provinces, two territories and four countries and been worn on stage at folk festivals in Dawson City, Vancouver, Winnipeg, Antigonish, Yellowknife and many other locations. Someone even knitted a tiny version for his young son. One day someone will write a book about the adventures of this legendary sweater!

Sam Barksy

In 2017, Baltimore-based knitter Sam Barsky made headlines worldwide when it was discovered that he was knitting sweaters that featured famous landmarks and then was travelling to those locations to take selfies! Sam has taken his freestyle-knit sweaters to places such as The Golden Gate Bridge in San Francisco, Times Square in New York City, Stonehenge in England and the Eiffel Tower in Paris,

France, just to name a few. His heart-warming story has been shared by everyone from NPR to *The Times of Israel* and everyone in between!"

Film and Television Inspired Knitting

Sometimes films and television shows inspire knitting projects on a huge scale. Here are ten popular examples of TV shows that have inspired an army of knitters to take up their needles:

1. **Doctor Who:** You've no doubt seen many patterns for the Doctor's famous scarf – there are many variations to accommodate specific seasons/versions. You'll also find Dalek inspired mittens and dresses, and TARDIS blanket, socks and *amigurumi*, even baby clothes – this show is a very popular source of knitting inspiration. The prize for the most odd design goes to certifiably obsessed Whovian Teryn Pierce for her "Ood Snood" pattern, which is available free at her site, "ThriftRedHead".

2. **Outlander:** Claire Fraser is a nurse, later a doctor, and a time-traveller who has lived both in the 20th century and the 18th century. The first season inspired many collections of period-piece designs.

3. **Hunger Games:** Katniss Everdeen's one-shouldered cowl-neck wrap from *Catching Fire* is still a popular item to knit (or crochet). You'll

find dozens of variations on Ravelry.

4. **Star Wars:** Everything from popsicle cosies, to Princess Leia wigs for cospay – if it's related to Star Wars in any way, there is a pattern in the galaxy somewhere, and probably not far, far away either.

5. **Game of Thrones:** Winter is coming … so what better thing to do than start knitting? This series has inspired everything from *amigurumi*, to dragon scale gloves, scarves, pillows, illusion-knits, shawls, blankets, hats, cowls, socks and more. It's a very popular show to knit to …

6. **Harry Potter:** Another popular pattern-spawning franchise, you'll easily find a wide variety of garments related to Harry Potter. Scarves, hats, blankets, bookmarks, mandrakes, dolls, slippers and more … it's a cosplayer's dream come true.

7. **Downton Abbey:** Set in 1912, this British drama follows the lives of the Crawley family and its servants. Ravelry users have shared dozens of patterns inspired by the show, many featuring lace and delicate ornate embellishments – the cloche hat, a fitted, bell-shaped hat for women that was invented in 1908 by milliner Caroline Reboux, is a popular example.

8. **Lord of the Rings:** Peter Jackson's epic trilogy is the go-to inspiration for intricate lace shawls, socks, even Dwarven battle helmets. You can also find charts for the famous "one ring to rule them

all" inscriptions, written in Elvish, of course.

9. **The Minions:** Phone cases, dolls, hats, yellow ones, purple ones – these strange banana-loving creatures from the *Despicable Me* franchise have inspired an army of knitters to take up their needles.

10. **All Superhero Cinematic Universes:** It doesn't matter whether you prefer DC over Marvel, Batman over Spiderman, if you're a knitter (or crocheter), the universe we live in has got you covered. You'll find hundreds, if not thousands, of colourful patterns for things like highly-detailed cosplay gear, *amigurumi*, graphgans and corner-to-corner (C2C) blankets, hats, mitts, scarves, a variety of weaponry and so much more.

HONOURABLE MENTION: "My Neighbor Totoro", a 1988 Japanese animation written and directed by Hayao Miyazaki (Studio Ghibli) is the inspiration for many knitted toys, dolls, jumpers and mittens – I've even seen a Totoro-shaped needle gauge! Tiny Totoro hats are quite trendy and nerdy knitters like to put them on creatures from other franchises, such as Minions and characters from the game Pokemon Go.

Knitting in Pop Culture Today

"If you're having purl problems, I feel bad for you son … I got 99 problems but a stitch ain't one … "

Knitting In Music

In 1992, American-Canadian artist Meryn Cadell released an album called *Angel Food For Thought* and its first single was a catchy little Top 40 ditty called *The Sweater*. A spoken word monologue with a swanky backing track, the song is about a girl who is obsessed with a boy whose sweater she has borrowed during a camping trip. Alas, the love is unrequited, the sweater must be returned but our protagonist prevails when she sees the label on the sweater: "100 per cent Acrylic". Ouch. And squeaky.

This song, popular on campus and alternative radio in North America, allegedly prompted the band Weezer to respond with the song *Undone – The Sweater Song* and went on to be one of their biggest hits. Even today, both of these songs are often featured back to back.

Sidebar: The Sweater Curse

Now is probably a good time to ask, do you know

about the "sweater curse"? The legend goes as follows: if a knitter gives a hand-knitted sweater to a significant other too soon, it will lead to the recipient breaking up with the knitter. Some go even further and say that the relationship is doomed to fail before the sweater is even finished! Is it just a silly superstition? You'll have to decide that one for yourself ...

Another interesting intersection of music and knitting occurred when Icelandic composer Hafdís Bjarnadóttir noticed the similarities between György Ligeti's *Atmosphères* and the pattern for a lace-based shawl. Inspired, she wrote her own score, *Thordis' Fichu*, which cleverly uses holes in knitting patterns to create pauses in the music. Bjarnadóttir's unusual methodology made headlines in the classical music world in 2013.

HONOURABLE MENTION:

Mike Nesmith's knitted wool hat ... Hey, hey, we're the Monkees!

Knitting in Pop Culture Today

"If you don't knit, bring a book."

Dorothy Parker

Knitting in Literature

Knitting appears in literature quite often as it can symbolise so many things – women's work, tradition, falling apart ("unraveling"), creative process, desire for authenticity, two things coming together, death and so much more.

Probably the most famous example of knitting in literature comes by way of Madame Defarge in Charles Dickens' *A Tale of Two Cities*. During the French Revolution, she sits by the guillotine, recording the names of beheaded enemies in wool. As mentioned earlier in the book, it's quite likely that Dickens took some liberty and embellished the story of the famed *tricoteuses* for literary effect.

Dickens' novel *David Copperfield* also features knitter Clara Peggotty, a housekeeper who provides motherly support and guidance to the book's namesake character, David.

Surprisingly, knitting also appears in Joseph

Conrad's disturbing novel, *Heart of Darkness*. Before Marlowe is sent to the Congo, he is greeted by two ladies knitting black wool, one old and one young, "guarding the door of Darkness."

It seems everyone is absorbed in their needlework in the Harry Potter novels by J.K. Rowling. Knitters from the series include Mrs. (Molly) Weasley, Ron Weasley's mom, Rubeus Hagrid, Sybill Trelawney, Dobby the house-elf, Hermione Granger, Albus Dumbledore and Minerva McGonagall.

Here are five other famous knitters depicted in classic and popular literature:

1. Jane Fairfax in *Emma* by Jane Austen (knitting also appears in Persuasion)
2. Miss Marple from the works of Agatha Christie
3. Penelope from *The Odyssey* by Homer
4. The Once-ler from *The Lorax* by Dr. Seuss
5. *Anne of Green Gables* by Lucy Maud Montgomery features numerous instances of knitting and crochet, so much so that in 2013 Joanna Johnson was inspired to release a book of patterns inspired by the series, *Green Gable Knits*.

If you're interested in more examples of knitting in literature – there are hundreds! – I recommend seeking out a web resource called "Wool Works".

HONOURABLE MENTION:

Not about knitting but worthy of a mention ...
published in 2013, "Crocheting With Kurt Cobain" by
Olive Collins is a short novel about a young woman
named Judith Wells — she's a deceased 21-year-
old celeb-obsessed Kurt Cobain fan who has to
relive her short life to atone for her wrongdoings. I
enjoyed it and am happy to say, go on, give it a read.

Knitting in Pop Culture Today

"I watch 'Mad Men,' I knit scarves, I cook and am very, very normal. Honestly."

Annie Lennox

Knitting in Advertising and Commercials

Over the last few years, knitting has become more and more prominent in mainstream advertising. Here are ten recent campaigns, all featuring knitting or crochet. For the purists reading this, yes, some of it may be computer-generated.

1. In 2012, Jessie Hemmons, aka ishknits, appears in a cheerful print ad for Tampax, alongside a yarn bombed bicycle, presumably created by her!
2. In 2013, Toyota worked with UK yarnbombers, Deadly Nightshade and The Fastener, to support Toyota's Positive campaign promoting hybrid vehicles. The installation appeared that April in the Brixton, London.
3. In 2014, Y&R in China launched an ad for Penguin Audiobooks. Based on the insight that knitters will often listen to audio books while knitting, the ad featured an over-the-shoulder view of a woman knitting ornate hand-writing

into her piece, symbolising the book she was listening to while knitting.

4. The Belgian Natural Gas Association has produced two memorable stop-motion commercials which feature houses, flowers and animals slowly becoming yarn bombed.

5. In 2014, sister duo Lorna and Jill Watt, aka "Knits For Life" were commissioned by Old Navy to yarn bomb bumper cars at their flagship stores in San Francisco and New York City. The red and white designs prominently featured the Norwegian-inspired selburose motif!

6. In 2014, a Delivery.com television commercial called "Strange Hobbies" featured a young guy "knitting" and explaining that the service gives him more time to enjoy his hobby. Eventually everything is covered in yarn, including him and his girlfriend. Here's the thing though, it's mostly crochet! Personally, I'm not a stickler when people make the wrong differentiation, but many people are … big faux pas!

7. In 2014, a Tim Horton's coffee shop in Fort Frances, Ontario (Canada) was covered in knitting, both on the inside and out! The stunt was so popular, it was reported in newspapers worldwide.

8. In 2015, renowned yarn bomber London Kaye executed the first fully crocheted billboard to be mounted in Times Square, New York City. For

years it was a dream of mine to see this kind of large-scale project mounted, so I was delighted when London invited me to work behind the scenes to secure the nearly 44 miles of yarn she needed for her and her team. 300,000 stitches later, what I believe to be the first fully fibre-based billboard, was born!

9. In 2015, yarn bomber Magda Sayeg worked with SKYY Vodka to create large-scale knitted Christmas ornaments which were displayed in Union Square in New York City. The installation also included a fleet of knit-wrapped, vintage pickup trucks.

10. In late 2016, Polish-born artist Olek unveiled a fully-crocheted billboard in support of Hillary Clinton's bid for the United States Presidency. Featuring Clinton's face and the hashtag #ImWithHer, the art piece was stitched together with help of 38 volunteers who assisted with the 94,880 stitches!

HONOURABLE MENTIONS: In 2006 a Gene Simmons look-a-like from the rock band KISS is seen knitting in a print ad for Hi-Fi Klubben; and in 2016, prolific knitter and rising YouTuber Kristy Glass was commissioned by MTV to knit holiday stockings resembling artists such as Sia and Justin Beiber.

Knitting in Pop Culture Today

"I did this scene in 'Lars and the Real Girl' where I was in a room full of old ladies who were knitting, and it was an all-day scene, so they showed me how. It was one of the most relaxing days of my life."

Ryan Gosling

Knitting Trends

You may not think of knitting as an activity that evolves much but it does and rather quickly! From patterns to yarns to art, knitting has its own culture that ebbs and flows alongside the times we live in.

Yarn Bombing

Yarn bombing is a type of street art that uses yarn or fibre rather than paint, chalk or paste-ups. Some people have taken exception to the name "yarn bomb", so you'll often find this art form described using other names such as yarn storming, guerrilla knitting, kniffiti, urban knitting or graffiti knitting. It's origins are often attributed to Magda Sayeg, a Houston-based artist who says she got the idea to yarn bomb a door handle in 2005.

Today yarn bombing is a worldwide phenomenon that has gained mainstream acceptance with installations popping up in cities all over the world. International Yarn Bombing Day happens on the 11th June each year.

Ten Famous Yarn Bombers To Check Out

1. Olek, USA
2. London Kaye, USA
3. Eric Rieger (HOTTEA), USA
4. Jessie Hemmons (ishknits), USA
5. Jane Balke Andersen (Queen Babs), Australia
6. Lauren O'Farrell (Deadly Knitshade), UK
7. Magda Sayeg (Knitta Please), USA
8. Nina Dodd (The Duke of Woolington), UK
9. Stephen Duneier (Yarnbomber), USA
10. Raquel Rodrigo, Spain

HONOURABLE MENTIONS: Victoria Villasana collaborates with street artists in London's East End neighbourhood of Shoreditch by adding striking embroidered elements to paste-ups. Her stitchwork focuses on geometric shapes and is very colourful. Madrid's Spidertag also plays with geometric shapes, using nails to secure his large-scale designs. Initially focused on yarn, he's currently experimenting with neon.

Ten Yarn Bombs Worth Remembering

1. Mexico City Bus Project in Mexico City – Magda Sayeg (2008)
2. Wall Street Bull in New York City – Olek (2010)
3. R2D2 Walkway Slipcover in Bellingham, WA – Sarah Rudder (2012)
4. DC-3 in Whitehorse, Canada – Yarn Bomb Yukon (2012)
5. Monster Benches in San Francisco, CA – Knits For Life (2014)
6. #BlackLivesMatter in Los Angeles, CA – Yarn Bombing Los Angeles (2015)
7. Witch Legs in Pittsburgh, PA – Rayna Noel (2016)
8. 67 Blankets for Nelson Mandela Day in South Africa – Nelson Mandela Foundation (2016) *
9. Klimt Painting in Prague – Eva Blahova (2016)
10. Ezra Jack Keats' Snowy Day in New Jersey – Hi, Jenny Brown (2017)

* This installation also holds the current Guinness World Record for largest hand knitted, non-crocheted blanket, measuring 1,378.28 m² (14,835.68 ft²).

HONOURABLE MENTIONS: Knit the Bridge's yarn bomb of the Andy Warhol Bridge in Pittsburgh, Pennsylavnia featured over 600 knitted and crocheted blankets, representing work from over 1,800 knitters and crocheters.

The Ugly Christmas Jumper

Based on the stereotype that our family members love to give us ugly hand-knitted jumpers as gifts for Christmas, the ugly christmas jumper phenomenon as a pop culture trend has really come into its own in the last few years. In fact, you may even say it's a tradition as every year people around the world gather to show off the ugliest christmas jumper they can make or find at the thrift shop. Popular embellishments include LED lights and eyelash glitter yarn – the more the merrier. There's even a National Ugly Christmas Jumper Day on the third Friday of December in the US and Christmas Jumper Day in the UK is organised by Save the Children to raise money for charity.

Knitting Memes

When knitters found out that Ryan Gosling learned how to knit on the set of *Lars and the Real Girl*, it set off a frenzy of LOL-style memes. Taking their cue from the already-established Ryan Gosling Tumblr blog (Fuck Yeah! Ryan Gosling), each meme started with "Hey girl" and ended with some fantasy notion only a knitter would wish for ...

- Hey girl, I'm bummed they took down your yarn bomb too.
- Hey girl, I saw that one of your skeins was the wrong dye lot, and got the right one for you.

- Hey girl, can I give you a hand massage? You've been knitting for six hours.

And so on … Of course, Gosling is not the only celebrity to be pulled into this fibre fantasy world – similar memes involve George Clooney, Morgan Freeman, Jude Law and others.

In general, knitting memes are a very popular trend and often feature puns or re-imaginings of popular quotes and phrases. You may have noticed that I've included several throughout this book!

Temperature Scarves

The concept is simple: it's a knit or crochet pattern that's created over the course of a year with colour changes based entirely on temperature ranges. To get started, choose your colours, then assign each colour to a set of temperature values. As the weather changes day to day, knit or crochet a row based on the range/colour combination you designated. Some folks have even applied this concept to their favourite sports team's performance over a season!

Knitting And Crochet Cruises

Cruises for fibre enthusiasts have exploded in popularity over the last decade. Japan, China, Alaska, Hawaii, Panama, and Antarctica are just a few of the places you can travel to while enjoying the company of fellow fibre enthusiasts. Offered by a variety of cruise lines, knitting cruises offer the opportunity to travel and to improve skills at the same time. Most speciality cruises of this nature feature workshops with well-known instructors and designers, often the most sought-after in the yarn world.

Cosplay

Costume play, aka "cosplay," is the practice of dressing up as a character from a favourite movie, book, or video game. More and more, knitting and crochet is represented in many cosplayers' get-ups. In one of the most famous examples, well-known cosplayer Summer Murphy, better known as "Fangirl Physics," knitted a full-body Captain America costume that fans still rave about today!

Knitting Records

1. **Most people knitting simultaneously:** 3,083 in an event organised by the National Federation of Women's Institutes (UK), in London on 30 May 2012.
2. **Largest sculpture, knitted:** The Gelatin Collective (Austria) created a 61-m (200-ft) long pink knitted rabbit on the side of a mountain in Piedmont, northern Italy. It took more than a year to knit the basic shape and a further seven weeks to stuff and place it.

3. **Largest knitted hat:** 20.2 m (66 ft 3.2 in) in circumference, made by Industrias Textiles de Sudamerica (Peru) as measured in Lima, Peru, in April of 2015.
4. Longest knitted scarf: 4,565.46 m (14,978 ft 6.16 in) long, made by Helge Johansen (Norway), in Oslo, Norway, verified on 12 November 2013.
5. Largest knitting needles: 3.98 m (13 ft 0.75 in) long with a diameter of 8.25 cm (3.25 in). They were made by Jim Bolin (USA), measured on 20 May 2013.

Craft + Activism = "Craftivism"

The term "craftivism" was coined by Betsy Greer in 2003. A journalist and craftivist herself, she defines the term as follows, "Craftivism is a way of looking at life where voicing opinions through creativity makes your voice stronger, your compassion deeper and your quest for justice more infinite."

Especially popular within feminist circles, recent craftivist projects include:

☆ **The Pussy Hat Project** – Co-founded by Krista Suh and Jayna Zweiman, discussed in more detail in section one of this book.
☆ **March For Science Hats** – Similar to the Pussy Hat Project, but for science! Patterns include: Resistor Hat by Stanford microbiologist Heidi

Arjes; GENIE DNA hat by biochemist Rebecca Roush Brown; Ocean Beanie by Joan Rowe.

☆ **You Are So Very Beautiful** – Public art project of hand-stitched affirmations left in public places, organised by Betsy Greer.

☆ **The Snatchel Project** – in 2012, American knitters and crocheters were encouraged to send a knit or crochet vagina or uterus to a male Senator or Congressional Representative with the message, "Hands off my uterus! Here's one of your own!"

Knitting in Pop Culture Today

"Keep calm and carry yarn... "

Knitting Controversies

Knitting is not without its fair share of controversies. We are a fighting bunch! Here are three significant conflicts that have rocked the world of yarn over the past few years ...

The Ravelrympics Get Shut Down

In June 2012, the US Olympic Committee sent a cease-and-desist to Ravelry users who organised the "Ravelympics", an online event founded in 2006 in which knitters and crocheters challenged themselves to complete projects in games like "sock put".

Citing that the event name was in violation of the Olympic trademark, the strongly-worded letter caused an uproar among Ravelympics supporters, causing the hashtag #ravelympics to trend on Twitter.

Eventually the Committee apologised: "While we stand by our obligation to protect the marks and terms ... we sincerely regret the use of insensitive terms in relation to the actions of a group that was clearly not intending to denigrate or disrespect the Olympic Movement."

Since then, organisers changed the event name to the "Ravellenic Games."

"Casting Off My Womb"

In 2013, performance artist Casey Jenkins decided to use knitting to challenge the negative and fearful view many have of the female genitalia. For 28 days, the same length as the average menstrual cycle, Jenkins sat in a gallery in Australia and knitted a long scarf from white wool inserted in her vagina. The term "vaginal knitting", first coined by Australian TV channel SBS2Australia, made headlines around the world, prompting many to object to Jenkins's project.

Olek's Underwater Yarn Bomb in Mexico

In 2014, crochet artist and yarn bomber Agata Oleksiak, aka Olek, covered British artist Jason deCaires Taylor's famous underwater sculptures at the Cancun Underwater Museum in Mexico in biodegradable yarn. Inspired by Taylor's suggestion that the ocean's health is a "ticking time bomb", Olek says her intent was to further raise awareness about the plight of endangered sea creatures. The museum did not approve of Olek's yarn bomb and even went as far as to suggest a lawsuit against her.

No stranger to controversy, Olek would be in the news again two years later when she placed a lacy gas mask on a large sculpture of King Neptune at the Oceanfront of Virginia Beach on the East coast of the United States. Part of a larger installation for the Virginia Museum of Contemporary Art (MOCA), Olek said the mask was to symbolise the dangers of pollution for everyone, even a king like Neptune.

MOCA officials who commissioned the piece said they hadn't approved the mask and had city workers take it down when Olek refused to comply.

7. Knitter's Resources

"That's what I do ... I knit and I know things."

13 Websites Every Knitter Needs To Know

1. Ravelry – www.ravelry.com
2. Etsy – www.etsy.com
3. Craftsy – www.craftsy.com
4. Knitter's Review – www.knittersreview.com
5. Knitty – www.knitty.com
6. YouTube – www.youtube.com
7. Vogue Knitting – www.vogueknitting.com
8. Twist Collective – www.twistcollective.com
9. amirusi – www.amirisu.com
10. Pom Pom Quarterly – www.pompommag.com
11. Interweave – www.hinterweave.com
12. Rowan – www.knitrowan.com
13. Fringe Association – www.fringeassociation.com

Knitter's Resources

"Properly practised, knitting soothes the troubled spirit, and it doesn't hurt the untroubled spirit either."

Elizabeth Zimmerman

Charities That Want Your Knitting

I noted this before and will again … please, please, please double check with a charity before you send your handmade donation. As of the date of publication, this list is current BUT … knitters are a very generous bunch and many times an organisation who puts a call out for donations will get absolutely inundated. Sometimes they get so many donations that they don't know what to do … so as not to discourage you, just check beforehand so that your generosity goes to where it's needed the most!

In addition to the specific projects below, consider reaching out to local organisations such as churches, charity shops, legions, homeless shelters, women's safe spaces, hospitals, schools, youth programmes, birthing centres and more. They often need hats, socks, sweaters and scarves.

Afghans for Afghans
Age UK
Algerian Action
Alice's Embrace
Apostleship of the Sea
Archie Project
Association of Youth Ministry Educators
Baby Bird Nest Craft-Along
Battersea Dog and Cats homes
Binky Patrol
Bliss
Blythswood Care
Bristol Knititiative
Bundles of Love
Calvin's Hats
Care Wear Volunteers, Inc.
Cats Protection
Cherished Gowns for Angel Babies
Christmas at Sea
Cuddles UK
Delaware Head Huggers
Doctors Without Borders / Médecins Sans Frontières
Dogs Trust
Dulaan Project
Elephants Remember Joplin
Feel Better Friends
Francis House
Freedom From Fistula Foundation
Get Sirius

Halos of Hope

Hand in Hand for Syria

Handmade Especially For You

Hats 4 Heroes

Hat Box Foundation

Headway

Hope and Aid Direct

International Aid Trust

Izzy Dolls (HPIC)

Kirsty's Kids

Knit For Kids

Knit for Nowt' Yorkshire

Knit For Peace

Knit Your Bit

Knit-a-Square

KnitAid

Knitted Knockers

Knitting and Giving

Knitting Rays of Hope

Knots of Love

L.I.L.Y (Love in the Language of Yarn) – Syria

Leggings for Life

Life After Loss

Lisa's Stars

Little Yellow Duck Project

Lucy Ladybug Knit-Along

Mats for Cats

Mission To Seafarers

Mother Bear Project

Muddy Footprint

Mylo and His Friends Supporting Burnley NICU

National Animal Welfare Trust

Needles & Hooks, Angels & Preemies

Nimble Fingers on the Prairie

Operation Gratitude

Operation Orphan

Palliative Care Prayer Shawl Project

Patterns for Change

Precious Pals Program

Project Linus

Project Peru

Re-Act Lochabar

Red Scarf Project

Sands UK

Siblings Together

SIMBA – Simpson's Memory Box Appeal

Snuggles Project

Spana

SSPCA / RSCPA / WSPCA

St. Mungo's

The Highlands Support Refugees

Warm Up America!

WildCare's Baby Bird Nest Campaign

Wildlife Victoria

Wooly Hugs

Women In Need

Wrapped in Hugs

Yarns of Hope Charity

Knitter's Resources

"Might as well face it, you're addicted to yarn..."

Knitting Abbreviations

If you want to read a knitting pattern successfully, here are the essential acronyms:

* ❀ [ ] – work instructions within brackets as many times as directed
* ❀ " – inch(es)
* ❀ ( ) – work instructions within parentheses in the place directed
* ❀ * * – repeat instructions following the asterisks as directed
* ❀ * – repeat instructions following the single asterisk as directed
* ❀ alt – alternate
* ❀ approx – approximately
* ❀ beg – begin/beginning
* ❀ bet – between
* ❀ BO – bind (cast) off
* ❀ CA – colour A
* ❀ CB- colour B
* ❀ CC – contrasting colour
* ❀ cm – centimetre(s)

- ✿ cn – cable needle
- ✿ CO – cast on
- ✿ cont – continue
- ✿ dec – decrease/decreases/decreasing
- ✿ dpn – double pointed needle(s)
- ✿ fl – front loop(s)
- ✿ foll – follow/follows/following
- ✿ g – gram
- ✿ inc – increase/increases/increasing
- ✿ k or K – knit
- ✿ k2tog – knit 2 stitches together
- ✿ kwise – knitwise
- ✿ LH – left hand
- ✿ lp(s) – loop(s)
- ✿ m – metre(s)
- ✿ M1 – make one stitch
- ✿ M1 p-st – make one purl stitch
- ✿ MC – main colour
- ✿ mm – millimetre(s)
- ✿ oz – ounce(s)
- ✿ p or P – purl
- ✿ p2tog – purl 2 stitches together
- ✿ pat(s) or patt – pattern(s)
- ✿ pm – place marker
- ✿ pop – popcorn
- ✿ prev – previous
- ✿ psso – pass slipped stitch over
- ✿ pwise – purlwise
- ✿ rem – remain/remaining
- ✿ rep – repeat(s)

- ❀ rev St st – reverse stockinette stitch
- ❀ RH – right hand
- ❀ rnd(s) – round(s)
- ❀ RS – right side
- ❀ sk – skip
- ❀ sk2p – slip 1, knit 2 together, pass slip stitch over the knit 2 together;
- ❀ skp – slip, knit, pass stitch over—one stitch decreased
- ❀ sl – slip
- ❀ sl st – slip stitch(es)
- ❀ sl1k – slip 1 knitwise
- ❀ sl1p – slip 1 purlwise
- ❀ ss – slip stitch (Canadian)
- ❀ ssk – slip, slip, knit these 2 stiches together—a decrease
- ❀ sssk – slip, slip, slip, knit 3 stitches together
- ❀ st(s) – stitch(es)
- ❀ St st – stockinette stitch/stocking stitch
- ❀ tbl – through back loop
- ❀ tog – together
- ❀ WS – wrong side
- ❀ wyib – with yarn in back
- ❀ wyif – with yarn in front
- ❀ yd(s) – yard(s)
- ❀ yfwd – yarn forward
- ❀ yo – yarn over
- ❀ yon – yarn over needle
- ❀ yrn – yarn around needle

Podcasts

One thing that's great about knitting is that it allows you to do something productive while indulging in your favourite shows – win-win! I love bingeing on my favourite television shows and films while getting a few rows in. Lately I've been adding podcasts to the mix and I'm always surprised at the variety of niche topics out there. Whatever pings your pong, there's a podcast for you. The ones I have chosen are predominantly American, but choose your favourites wherever you live. Here are five of my own suggestions that may help you along with your stitches.

1. **This American Life** – hosted by Ira Glass, this show has been around forever and it truly never disappoints. It covers a wide range of human interest stories, often from the least-expected places.

2. **Sawbones: A Marital Tour of Misguided Medicine** – hosted by Dr. Sydnee McElroy and her husband Justin, these two talk about medical history and all the terrifying (yes, terrifying) ways medical professionals have tried to "heal" patients over the years. Gross-out factor is high on this one – love it!

3. **The Nerdist** – Chris Hardwick is the real deal. His

interview style is disarming and as such he's able to have intimate and entertaining conversations with the most beloved nerdy celebs.

4. **They Walk Among Us** – Another fab husband and wife team, Benjamin and Rosie are true crime enthusiasts who explore the sinister and the surreal of UK crimes. Perfect to stitch to …

5. **The Allusionist** – Presented and produced by Helen Zaltzman in bite-size bits of 15 minutes, this podcast is perfect for word nerds who have a few minutes to get few rows in before moving onto life's next big challenge.

Bonus podcast: Anything produced by The Kitchen Sisters, Davia Nelson & Nikki Silva. Hat tip to my good friend Michael Burtt for turning me onto these amazing storytellers.

And here is a round-up of some of the most popular knitting audio/video podcasts:

A Playful Day	Caithness Craft Collective
Actually Knitting	Cast On
Along The Lanes	CLN Podcast
AndreSueKnits	CogKNITive
Bakery Bears Podcast	Commuter Knitter

Curious Handmade

Dancing Geek

Doubleknit

Down Cellar Studio

Electric Sheep

Elise Gets Crafty

Fruity Knitting

Geeky Girls Knit

Hollywood Knitter

Hue Loco

Inside Number 23

Just One More Row

Knit British

2 Knit Lit Chicks

Knit 1 Geek 2

Knit.fm (archives)

Knitcircus

Knitmore Girls

Knitting Expat Podcast

Knitting Pipeline

Knitting Rose Podcast

Kristy Glass Knits

Little Bobbins Knits

Little Yellow Uke Crafts

Louleigh

Never Not Knitting
   (archives)

Pins and Needles

Pom Pom Quarterly

Savvy Girls

Shinybees

Sockmatician

Stitched Together
   (archives)

Susan B Anderson

The Anatomy of Knitting

Creative Yarn
   Entrepreneur

The Fawn Knits

The Furry Knitter

Grocery Girls Knit

The Knit Girllls

The Spicy Homemaker

The Woolly Hub Podcast

The Yarniacs

Tilly Trout

Truly Myrtle

Very Pink Knits

Woolful

Yarn in the City

Yarn Thing With Marly Bird

Knitter's Resources

Teachers and Resources

Every year knitting faithfully shows up in the top 10 of "how-to" internet searches, so if you don't know how to do it, you're certainly not alone. If you're interested in learning, below are some resources to get you started.

5 Web Sites That Will Help You Learn How To Knit

1. Craftsy – www.craftsy.com
2. Knitting For All – www.knittingforall.com
3. Creative Bug – www.creativebug.com
4. YouTube – www.youtube.com
5. SkillShare – www.skillshare.com
6. TakeLessons – www.takelessons.com

Popular Knitting Instructors

From beginner how-to classes all the way to more advanced garment-making, knitters at any skill level will find something to learn from the amazing instructors listed below.

Amy Herzog	Ann Budd
Amy Singer	Ann McCauley
Andrea Wong	Anna Zilboorg
Aneeta Patel	Anne Berk
Angela Tong	Anne Hanson

Anne Kuo Lukito

Antje Gillingham

Aurora Sisneros

Barry Klein

Betsy Hershberg

Bristol Ivy

Brooke Nico

Caddy Melville Ledbetter

Candace Eisner Strick

Carol Feller

Carol Sulcoski

Cat Bordhi

Chris Bylsma

Cindy Craig

Clara Parkes

Cornelia Tuttle Hamilton

Daniel Yuhas

Deborah Jarchow

Donna Druchunas

Edie Eckman

Eunny Jang

Fiona Ellis

Fiona Morris

Franklin Habit

Gayle Roehm

Ginger Luters

Gudrun Johnston

Gwen Bortner

JC Briar

Jean Frost

Jill Bigelow Suttell

Joyce Meader

Judy Pascale

Kate Gilbert

Kellie Nuss

Laura Bryant

Laura Nelkin

Leslye Solomon

Lily Chin

Lorilee Beltman

Lucy Neatby

Margaret Fisher

Marly Bird

Mary Jane Mucklestone

Meg Swansen

Melissa Leapman

Merike Saarniit

Myra Wood

Nancy Marchant

Patty Lyons

Renée Callahan

Sally Melville

Sandi Rosner

Sarah Eyre

Sarah Peasley

Stacey Trock

Stephen West

Susan B. Anderson

Susan Guagliumi   Tanis Gray
Susanna Hansson   Vickie Howell
Tamara Kelly

Important Dates for Knitters and Wool Festivals Around the World

All around the world and throughout the year, knitters and fibre enthusiasts gather to attend sheep and wool festivals, cruises, knitting retreats, and various consumer trade shows. Clara Parkes maintains a decent listing of worldwide events through her Knitter's Review web site located at www.knittersreview.com/upcoming_events.

Some regular yearly highlights include:

JANUARY
Vogue Knitting Live, New York City, USA
Waltham Abbey Wool Show, Essex, UK
National NeedleArts Association Winter Trade Show, San Jose, USA

FEBRUARY
Unravel, Farnham, UK
Stitches West, Santa Clara, USA

MARCH
Spring Knitting & Stitching Show, London, UK
Yarn Ramble, Tasmania, Australia

Edinburgh Yarn Festival, Edinburgh, Scotland, UK
Vogue Knitting Live, Las Vegas, USA

APRIL

Wonderwool Wales, Llanelwedd, Builth Wells, Powys,
    Wales
The Knitting & Stitching Show, Edinburgh, Scotland,
    UK

MAY

London Craft Week, London, UK
Sheep's Head Yarn Festival, West Cork, Ireland
Woolfest Auckland, Auckland, New Zealand

JUNE

Leeds Wool Festival, Leeds, UK
World Wide Knit in Public Day (dates vary by region)
International Yarn Bombing Day

JULY

Blossom & Yarn: A Knitting and Flower Festival,
    Norfolk, UK
Annual British Wool Show, North Yorkshire, UK
Australian Sheep & Wool Show, Victoria, Australia

AUGUST

Stitches Midwest, Schaumburg, USA
Yarnfolk, Festival of Wool, Northern Ireland

SEPTEMBER
Kitchener-Waterloo Knitters' Fair, Ontario, Canada
California Wool and Fiber Festival, Boonville, USA
Bergen Knitting Festival, Bergen, Norway

OCTOBER
King's County Fiber Festival, Brooklyn, NY
Nova Scotia Fibre Arts Festival, Northumberland,
    Canada
Knitting & Stitching Show, London, UK
New York State Sheep and Wool Festival, Rhinebeck,
    USA

NOVEMBER
Vogue Knitting Live, Seattle, USA
Knitting & Stitching Show, Dublin, Ireland
Festiwool: Yarn and Wool Fair, Hertfordshire, UK

DECEMBER
BUST Holiday Craftacular, New York, Los Angeles,
    Boston and London, UK

References

History of Knitting

A History of Hand Knitting – Richard Rutt

The History of Knitting – Sheep & Stitch

88-year-old Saskatoon Man Makes Thousands of Socks for Shelters – Julianne Hazlewood, CBC News

The D.I.Y. Revolutionaries of the Pussyhat Project – Rob Walker, The New Yorker

The Resistance Rises: How a March Becomes a Movement – Karl Vick, Time Magazine

How a Fractious Women's Movement Came to Lead the Left – Amanda Hess, New York Magazine

Weaving Vs. Knitting – Textilefashionstudy.com

Knitting 101 – Knitty.com

Atlas Obscura – Atlasobscura.com

Victoria and Albert Museum – Collections.vam.ac.uk

Bros and Rows: The Real History Of Men Who Knit – Huffingtonpost.com

QI: how knitting was used as code in WW2? – Telegraph.co.uk

History of Knitting – Makersmercantile.com

History of Hand Knitting – KCguild.org.uk

The History of Knitting Pt 2: Madonnas, Stockings and Guilds, Oh My! – Sheepandstitch.com

More knitting history: World War II – Judyweightman. wordpress.com

History of Knitting – Honorable Mention – CBC.ca

The Spy Who Knitted Socks – Rovingcrafters.com

Have knitting needles, will spy. Contact Molly Rinker, Philadelphia –Usedview.com

"Directions for Knitting Socks" – Agsas.org

Poppy knitters get a head start on appeal – Swindonadvertiser.co.uk

In the tower, the poppies flow: Inside an extraordinary art project –Macleans.ca

Tricoteuses: Knitting Women of the Guillotine –
    Geriwalton.com

Knitting Tools, Fibre and Jargon

Know Your Needles – Knitlikegranny.com
Why is the French shepherd knitting on stilts? – Heather-gill.
    blogspot.co.uk
Know Your Wools – Heddels.com
History of Wool – Quatr.us
Domestication of Sheep – Preceden.com
Quiviut – Arcticqiviut.com
Why Does a Vicuña Jacket Cost $21,000? – WSJ.com
What's softer – and more expensive – than a cashmere
    sweater? One made from qiviut, the fleece that's gathered
    and spun from the Alaskan musk ox – CSmonitor.com
About Suri Alpacas – Wildrosealpacas.com
Irene and Mr. Sheep – Imrsheep.com/index.html
Sheep 201 – Sheep101.info
Possum Yarn – Woolyarns.co.nz
History of Linen – Historyofclothing.com
Hemp Traders – Hemptraders.com
Nylon – Explainthatstuff.com
Pakucho – Trendsetteryarns.com
Rayon – Yarniapdx.com
Soy Silk – Dyeingtodye.tumblr.com
What is Tencel? – Ecomall.com
Sustainable fabric innovations – Thealternative.in
What is a skein? – Freshstitches.com
Turning Fibre Into Yarn: The Art Of Spinning –
    Offthegridnews.com
Lisa's List: 12 Yarn Ball Types and How to Knit with Them –
    Interweave.com
5 Things You Didn't Know About Your Wool Sweater –
    Rodalesorganiclife.com
Origin of the word spinster – Merriam-webster.com

Different Types of Knitting

Fair Isle vs Intarsia – Maggiesrags.com
Mathematical – Toroidalsnark.net
Millennial Craft-makers Embrace Arm Knitting – Rachel Dodes
The Institute for Figuring
The Home of Mathematical Knitting – Sarah Marie-belcastro
6 Math Concepts Explained by Knitting and Crochet – Lela
    Nargi, Mental Floss
I-cord Knitting: "I" Is for "Ingenious" – Kathleen Cubley,
    Interweave

Around the World in 80 Stitches

Interlaced Ambiguities: The Origins Of Aran Knitting –
    Pamela MacKenzie, USA Today
The Story of the Selbu Mitten (Selbuvotten) – Anette Broteng
    Christiansen, ThorNews
Sheep Farming – The Encyclopedia of New Zealand
Canada Knits: Craft and Comfort in a Northern Land –
    Shirley A. Scott
Knit Wit: 5 Things You Didn't Know About Canada's Beloved
    Cowichan Sweater – Nathalie Atkinson, The Globe and Mail
Peru – Twistcollective.com
Knitting and Weaving in Peru – Clothroads.com
Peru: A Stitch Sublime – Horizons.team.org
Knitting in Japan – Lknits.com
Knit Japan – Knitjapan.co.uk
Forget colouring in for adults... the new way to beat stress is
    creating toys out of felt – Dailymail.co.uk
Canada Knits – Collections.mun.ca
Cowichan Sweaters – Theglobeandmail.com
Iceland Knitting – Sites.google.com
History of Icelandic Knitting – Freyjawoolstore.com
5 5 Things You Didn't Know About Icelandic Wool –
    Whatson.is
The Iconic Icelandic Sweater: Past and Present –
    Huffingtonpost.com

Fisherman Sweater – Knittingcurmudgeon.blogspot.com
What's a Gansey – BBC.co.uk
Popular Gansey Myths – Ganseys.com
Falkland Islands Wool – Independentstitch.typepad.com
History of the Selbu Mitten – Sofn.com
Sheep Population New Zealand – Theguardian.com

Why Do People Knit?

No Idle Hands: The Social History of American Knitting –
    Anne L. MacDonald
Stitch 'n Bitch Nation – Debbie Stoller
Why Do People Knit – The Health Benefits – Well.blogs.
    nytimes.com
31 Ways Knitting and Crochet Will Change Your Life … and
    Make You Healthier – Lionbrand.com
Prayer Shawl Ministry – Shawlministry.com

Knitting in Pop Culture Today

David Babcock, Knitting Runner – Guinnessworldrecords.com
Unravelled: the Saga of Grant Lawrence's CBC Sweater –
    Grantlawrence.ca
Bill Cosby, His Sweaters, and the Man Who Made Them –
    Fashionista.com
Olek billboard – Nymag.com
Tim Hortons – Dailymail.co.uk
Knitting in Literature – Newyorker.com
Olek – Ecouterre.com and pilotonline.com

Knitter's Resources

Knitting Abbreviations Master List – Craft Yarn Council
Fibre Events – Knittersreview.com/upcoming_events

Let's close Knits & Pieces with a playful yarn bomb pattern that even a beginner knitter can do. Special thanks goes to Erika Barcott for giving me permission to share her iconic treesweater pattern!

TREESWEATER PATTERN BY ERIKA BARCOTT

Find a good tree, then find a good branch on the tree. Ideally, the sweater will sit at eye level, and will have only one "arm". This pattern is sized for a tree that is 7 inches in circumference with a 2 inch branch, and has at least 4 inches between the "arm" branch and the next one up.

GAUGE: 4 sts x 6 rows = 1 x 1 inches on US 8 / UK 6 / 5mm needles

YARN: Worsted weight yarn, acrylic is preferable.

DIRECTIONS

Body
1. CO 26 stitches and work 4 rows in k2p2 rib.
2. Increase 6 stitches across the row (*k2, kfb* 6 times). (32 sts.)
3. Knit for 2 more inches (total 3 inches).
4. Divide the stitches in half by putting 16 on a stitch holder (or spare DPN). Knit 6 rows on each half, then rejoin by putting all the stitches on one needle, and knitting all across. You should end up with a slit an inch and a half high. After knitting across, start your collar. For the pictured treesweater, I switched to reverse stockinette for 4 rows to make a mock turtleneck. You can also work the collar in garter stitch, k2p2 ribbing, or the collar of your choice.

Sleeve
1. CO 12 and knit 6 rows (or the desired length of sleeve).
2 Seam the length of the sleeve, then attach it to the slit.

ATTACHING THE TREESWEATER

1. Slip the sleeve over the branch, and stitch a mattress sleeve up the side.

If you're not able to easily pull the sleeve over the branch, you'll find alternative instructions via Erika's Ravelry page. For more of her great work, visit erikabarcott.com.